SHIT
HAPPENS!

SHIT
HAPPENS!

The Building of a Mining Empire

Leonard De Melt

SHIT HAPPENS!
THE BUILDING OF A MINING EMPIRE

iUniverse books may be ordered through booksellers or by contacting:

iUniverse
1663 Liberty Drive
Bloomington, IN 47403
www.iuniverse.com
1-800-Authors (1-800-288-4677)

ISBN: 978-1-5320-6263-6 (sc)
ISBN: 978-1-5320-6264-3 (e)

Print information available on the last page.

iUniverse rev. date: 11/12/2018

CONTENTS

CHAPTER 1

BUFFALO, MOVING OUR CAR ABOUT THE ROAD.

A dark cold night, the blustery wind, blowing the snow at my windshield, almost whiteout conditions. We should have stopped and taken a hotel room in Hay River, but we wanted to get to Yellowknife, before my favorite uncle, Dad's favorite brother-in- law passed away.

I was driving the Makenzie Highway, at this point near the village of Providence, North West Territories. My father was screaming, becoming very angry. I was laughing. How is this possible? How could he be so scared? The more I laughed the angrier he became. I realized I was not quieting him, but scaring him more. My home was now in Vancouver. I had left my home driving north. My father had a few years earlier, moved south, near the place of his birth and now lived in Fort Saint John, northern British Columbia. A hunter/ trapper all his life, my father had been described as a "mountain of a man" in the book, Denison's Arctic Ice Roads and numerous other books about the arctic and now he was blind and hysteric, that we were driving, creeping slowly through a herd of buffalo. I remembered how he had scared me in similar situations, in the bombardier, with herds of Caribou, those years before I came of school age.

I knew he was now blind, but I did not realize he could see so little, almost not at all. As I was coming up to the herd of buffalo on the road, I started to slow down. Dad asked me "Why are we slowing down?" Only then did I realize how blind he had become. "Dad, there is a herd of buffalo on the road, I have to slow down drive slowly through them."' These buffalo stood well above, weighed many times, the small car I was driving.

Dad responded, "no, no, turn around, go back to Providence, wait for morning, get the Game Warden. If any of these buffalo touch this little car, they will turn it over. If any of these buffalo charge the car, they will demolish it and us as well." I kept driving. Somehow, I felt. ok. The buffalo were milling around but not charging the car. Some were now, behind the car, both sides of the car, brushing against the car but not aggressively. I worked my way slowly through the herd. After about possibly 20 minutes that seemed like hours, I was through the herd. I could now speed up carry on towards my home town of Yellowknife. The town I was born and grew up in.

I had left Yellowknife after high school, only returning very occasionally to visit my mother, sisters, uncles and cousins. I had mostly lost track of people who were dear to me. Dad had called me up the previous week. "Len, Uncle Danny, is very sick and could pass away imminently." I want to see, him one more time before he passes away."

Uncle Danny was a heavy chain smoker. I remember going to their trailer, one evening last time I was in Yellowknife" Uncle Danny was mom's youngest brother, not much more than a teenager, when my siblings and I were growing up. He often played with us, taught me how to swim and numerous other things. Dad, went on to say "Len can you help me see him" After thinking, fly or drive, I decided on driving. Dad was blind, he needs someone with him. This way I too, could see uncle Danny. Driving, I could pick up dad in Fort Saint John and carry on to Yellowknife.

We arrived in Yellowknife the following morning. I dropped my Dad off, at Linda's the home of my youngest sister and drove onto my mother's home, where I spent the next few days. We phoned my oldest sister, half sister, same father, different mother. 5 years older than myself.

Uncle Danny, mom's youngest brother, half brother, same mother, different father. My oldest sister had married, was the wife of my Uncle Danny.

As is so often the case in the Arctic, I was related to my oldest half sister, Doris, by two chains. She, Doris, was my sister because we had the same father. She was married to my Uncle, Mom's brother, Danny, so by marriage, she was also my aunt.

We phoned Doris. "We arrived in Yellowknife, how is Uncle Danny? can we come over and visit"

"Yes," Doris answered, "but Danny is sleeping right now. Please come over this evening."

We had arrived in time. Uncle Danny was still alive. We visited as often as he could accept us during the next few days, and then I had to return to work. The drive back to Vancouver was mostly uneventful, we did see more buffalo, many more buffalo, but well off the road. About a week later, we received the news, Uncle Danny had passed away.

CHAPTER 2

EVER THE PRACTICAL JOKER

We were hunters and the summers we had a garden, we did not need money. Twenty-four (24) hour, summer sunlight, caused those vegetables, that would grow in the arctic, to grow very big.

Every village had a little white building with a red roof, the Hudson Bay Store. These little buildings were the biggest building in each village. Rocher River had one of these. I am sure Dad, never had 10 cents in his pocket, never had ten cents to his name. There were two hunts per year, each lasting about 3 months. After each hunt, "winter hunt" and "spring hunt" Dad would deposit his furs at the Hudson's Bay store, and each time we needed, sugar, coffee, guns, shells, those things we must buy, we signed against furs, we had on deposit.

Of course, they were no basements on our homes. Before building a cabin a hole, called a cellar, was dug, over which the cabin was built. Each cabin then had a trap door in the floor and stairs going down into the cellar. Putting the gardens vegetables in here, preserved the vegetables all winter long.

Uncle Danny was always the practical joker. We ate, what, we hunted. Wild rabbits were a delicacy.

Often, whenever Uncle Danny needed to one up me, he would ask me, If I remember the time I kissed the rabbit's ass. I guess this happened when I was about 2 years old, Mom would have been about 19 and uncle Danny was several years younger. Uncle Danny had come home, from hunting, had shot a rabbit. I guess he wanted to tease, antagonize his sister. I do not remember but he asked me many times, "Do you remember kissing the rabbit's ass?" By the time he arrived home, the rabbit had frozen and somehow, telling me it was good luck, encouraged me to kiss the rabbit's butt.

In Yellowknife, I guess, I was about 14, Uncle Danny had been teasing me, about the rabbit or likely something else, he was, ever the practical joker. Our three (3) room house, and an attic, where us 5 children slept. At each end of the attic, there was a window. A peaked roof, porch attached to the front of the house, made my little deck, when I wanted to sit in the sun, I would crawl out the window, onto the roof of the porch, one leg straddling each side of the peaked roof. This day I was looking for revenge, or playing a practical joke of my own. With a big smile on my face, I was sitting on top the porch, waiting for Uncle Danny or Auntie Doris to come out the front door. I had a big bucket of water in my hand. Not sure from where, anyhow, Dad saw me. He grabbed a big bucket of water of his own, quietly came up to the attic behind me. Splash, through, the window onto my back came the full bucket of water, along with a roar of laughter from me dad. I, soaking wet, lost the big smile on my face. I was the loser on that one.

CHAPTER 3

MY LEG, BADLY BURNT FELT LIKE IT WAS ON FIRE!

My earliest memory. I was 2 years old, would soon be three. I look at my scars, and it all comes back so vividly. We were living in Uncle Art's 2 room structure. A wall of logs separated the two rooms. A duplex of one room each. Uncle Ray and his wife, lived in one room.

Mom, Dad & I lived in the other room. Dad was a Trapper of Artic furs, Wolves, Foxes, Lynx, Wolverine etc. hence Dad was normally away, on the trap line. Winter hunt, Spring hunt etc. Spring hunt was mostly for Beaver and Muskrats.

My mother, like "most mothers, atta qualify for Sainthood." By the age of 24, mom had the 4 of us. My mother was 17 when I was born, so by now she would have been 19 years old. Our water came out of the river, breaking the ice and carrying it up to our cabin, our one room, by the pail. The room was heated by a wood stove in the center of the room. Mom bathed me and my baby brother, by hauling water up from the river, heating the water on the wood stove, and bathing us. To guard us against the cold. after bathing mom would dress us in long underwear. (long johns) The material of underwear in those days is not the material of today. I could not stand the itching of the underwear against my skin.

Mom went to dress me in the underwear. I did not want the itchy material against my shin. I squirmed out of her hands and ran away, round and round the red, hot stove in the center of the room. Mom tried to grab me but to late. My little two (2) year old right leg, fell against the side of the burning stove. The meat cooking could be smell throughout the room and into the adjoining room of my Aunt and Uncle.

"Mommy, help me!" I shrieked. There are no Doctors in the arctic. My screaming and the burning was intense. With time I did recover, but the scars remain.

Mom was likely as good a hunter, trapper as my father. My mom, from an early age, being raised along this river, never went to school, but she could shoot a rifle, set a fur trap as well as any man. In addition, she was an excellent seamstress. She could make any of the native, arctic clothing.

My mother completed taking care of me, as best she could and returned to her nightly task.

There were about 10 shacks in this village along the river.

My grandmother lived in one, some distance along from where we lived. I used to like visiting my grandmother. during the summers she always kept a garden. In the garden, she always had rhubarb growing. I do not know what she used for ingredients, but somehow, she was always able to make the best rhubarb pies. My grandmother was a great cook. Further along the river lived my mother's stepfather, the father of mom's youngest brother.

CHAPTER 4

WOLVES

In front of each shack, along this river was a fish rack. The transportation of the day, was Dog Team. Each Trapper had a team of 6 to 10 dogs. To feed 6 to 10 dogs over the winter took about 2000 fish. The Fish racks were made to hang fish out of the reach of the animals. Poles were stuck upright into the ground and then at about 10 feet high. horizontal poles were placed on the upright poles. A stick would be stuck through the head of the fish and hung on the horizontal poles. About 10 fish would hang from each of these Horizontal sticks. At night the wolves would come. The wolves would come and start jumping at these fish.

My father being away, it was my mothers job to protect these fish. Burned and very uncomfortable, I had stopped crying, my mother could return to her nightly task. My mother would open the door about 3 to 6 inches and shoot at the wolves. This would scare the "crap out of me!" My mother, although, still only 19 seemed much older to me. I knew she could protect me. Still, I never felt totally comfortable while mom had the door open, shooting at these wolves. I was never totally comfortable and yet at the some time challenged.

Within a few days, I was on the mend. Each time mom would want to put on this Itchy underwear I would challenge the stove. I would try to stay out of my mother's reach by running around and around the stove, but these times, keeping my distance.

In the spring of that year, my mother moved through the forest, some distance along the river, to live with her mother. My Father, was away from home, on the "Spring Hunt."

From a flat board, my Uncle Danny, had carved me a gun. Now I had my own gun. I believed I could shoot the wolves. To this day, my mother, proudly, tells the story again and again, and I enjoy her version, better than my own. With the hot sun and long days that come with spring in the arctic, near arctic, and most of the ice had melted off the river.

My mother and grandmother were in a frantic search, for me. They kept running up and down and along the river. Running to the other cabins along the river, "Had anyone seen Len?" They were certain I had drowned.

In desperation, mom guessed, "well, I will go back through the forest to the cabin where we had spent the winter, Len may have gone there." As mom started along the trail, I was coming back, wooden gun in hand. I guess you could call that my first hunt. I had gone looking for those wolves.

Walking with my head low. I was distraught. I had gone hunting for wolves and did not see any.

Mom, seeing me coming out of the bush, walking along the trail, did not know weather to laugh or cry. She did both. I did get so very many hugs from both my mother and my grandmother. I knew I was loved. My hunt was a failure, yet Mom and grandma were treating me like a hero. I was getting so many hugs and grandma's rhubarb pie. My hunt was a failure and yet, I was being treated like a hero!

I guess the most important thing, is, not that I failed, but that I tried.

Not understanding why, they were so glad to see me, was I thinking, "It is ok to fail, as long as I tried," my thoughts: perhaps not as clearly as that.

Yet, it surprised me, all of a sudden, I was feeling very good about myself, feeling very good that I had tried. Tried to hunt wolves.

For these many years, again and again, with pride in her voice, mom tells the story of my first hunt.

When mom tells the story, of my first hunt, it includes Dad. "Surely, I expected Dad would be there". "I had walked through the forest, to the old house, the house we had spent the winter, looking for my Dad, expecting my Dad would help me with bigger guns to hunt the wolves." Of course Dad was away on the "Spring Hunt" the old cabin was empty, No wolves jumping, trying to pull down the fish, Dad not being there, the cabin being vacant, I turned around and walked back to Grandma's cabin.

She was proud of her hunter, going to get those wolves, at the same time lecturing me, explaining to me that my gun was not adequate, about the quality of my gun. Fortunately for me, I did not see any wolves. My first hunt was unsuccessful, but that didn't stop. I have been hunting all my life, first for animals, later for mines.

CHAPTER 5

AN EDUCATION

My Grandfather would say, "A good man, does not need an education, a useless man, an education will not help." I am so very glad, my parents thought differently, that my dad thought differently than my grandfather.

Mom and dad, having not gone to school decided they wanted me to get an education. When I was 5 we moved to village of Rocher River, where there was a school. The village of Rocher River was a little bigger. Rocher River had about 40 cabins strung out along the river. Dad had a two, room cabin in Rocher River. There were two fur trading posts in Rocher River. Hudson's Bay Company had a small store/ trading post and my Dad's father also had a store/ trading post.

I turned 6 in January. The teacher in the one room school house, said now that I was 6, I could go to school. The teacher was a white woman, from down south. The one thing I can remember learning in that school was the song "Ten Little Indians".

In March, Dad decided, I was not learning anything. We had to move 100 miles across Great Slave Lake to the gold mining town of Yellowknife. Dad hitched up his team of 7 dogs.

Placed a 3-star eiderdown sleeping bag in the toboggan. I was placed in the sleeping bag at the front of the toboggan. My mother, and 4-year-old brother, Mike, also in the sleeping bag sat near the backboard, the back of the toboggan, and my father stood on the very back of the toboggan.

Mush! The dogs jumped forward. We were on our way to Yellowknife. It took us two days to get to Yellowknife. There were cabins on Outpost Island. We slept one night in these cabins.

After two days we arrived in Yellowknife. My mother, had been born in Fort Resolution, on the south side of Great Slave Lake, but I had been born in Yellowknife. My parents returned to the village immediately after I was born. Now I was back in the town of my birth. My grandfather, Ed De Melt had staked Yellowknife Con Mine in the early thirties.

In 1946 when I was born, the mine was a thriving entity. My grandfather had sold the claims for, near nothing, $5,000, which he split 4 ways, the people he had working for him. My grandfather kept back an NSR. (Net Smelter Return) which he also sold the following year. Our family had this opportunity, and basically "blew it".

Before my grandfather passed away, I asked him many times: "Why did you sell the NSR!?" My grandfather would answer: "I did not know the Mine was so rich. The CM&S, the forerunner of what is Teck Resources today, geologist told me, "there was no gold there" Over the next 50 years, more than 5 million ounces were mined from the Con Mine.

There where no additional monetary rewards but there were some recognition/ some perks: My mother at age 17, gave me birth in the Con Mine, First Aid Shack. I say "I was born in a mine and since, have been in mines everyday of my life." (I did miss those 6 years, we had returned to our village on the south side of Great Slave lake.)

Also, a street in Yellowknife has our family name.

After two days of «Dog Mushing» across Great Slave Lake, I was now about to be listed in Yellowknife Public School. We rented a small 2 room cabin, in what is know as the "Old Town" of part of Yellowknife. The "old town" has no plumbing, no running water, the poorest section of Yellowknife. Again, our occasional baths were in a steal tub, mom heated on the stove. I guess I smelled. The school kids took to calling me "De smelt." Instead of "De Melt", they would put a "s" in front of "melt" I was intimidated and shy. These were, to me, sophisticated kids from the south. The sons and daughters of the Miners and mine management, the sons and daughters of the local shop owners, the theatre, the son of the local Lawyer, the owner of the Newspaper News of the North" These kids were calling me "Smelt". When school year ended, June came, with only 3 months of school in Yellowknife, the teacher did not move me ahead that year. As it turned out I would be almost 8 years of age before, I would get another chance at some schooling.

CHAPTER 6

THE FIRST BOAT, THE BOMBARDIER.

Dad had to find work. Dad had no education and no saleable skills.

Minimum requirements, actually, no requirements for a Hunter/ Trapper in the town of Yellowknife. With the money Dad has saved from that winter's hunt, Dad bought a boat, something a little bigger than a large canoe, as it had an inboard motor and a bit of a cabin. Dad was able to get some work for this little boat, hauling groceries, fuel and men to the mining exploration camps that were springing up around Great Slave Lake.

That summer, the oldest of my sisters, Hazel was born. I did have an older half sister, from a different mother, Doris, whom I had not yet been told about.

One of the mining exploration camps was on Stark Lake, up a short river, from the east arm of Great Slave Lake. With his boat, dad kept this camp supplied until fall came, ice was forming on the lakes. What could dad do. The Ridley brothers, owners of this exploration camp owned a small bush plane and a Bombardier. (The original Bombardiers, which were enclosed, big doors on the sides and could haul a load larger than a one-ton truck.)

The Ridley Brothers would give Dad work but he had to move to the mining camp. Here I was out of school again. At the mining camp on Stark Lake, the company had built 2 building. One long one, for the Mine Manager and his wife, which one end doubled as a cook house.

One bunkhouse for the 4 miners.

They hired Dad to drive this bombardier, travel across the lake ice and keep the camp supplied...but they wanted Dad to move to the camp on Stark Lake. We were up-rooted, again. moved to Stark Lake. They had no cabin for us. Dad build a wooden floor and pitched a tent over this. We did have a wood stove in the corner. The fall winds would blow, coming off the long lake, seemed to aim directly for the opening in the door of our tent. The wood stove would burn out during the night. Close the tent flaps, door, as well as one could, still a small pile of snow near the door, would be in the tent before morning. At night I was sure the howling wind would lift our tent right off the tent frame. The snow would pile up around the tent, but now before howling and circling the tent at least 3 times.

I was still 6 when we arrived in Stark Lake. The lake froze over and the caribou came. At times caribou would be crossing the lake ice some distance down the lake, seemed to be thicker than mosquitoes. There were caribou everywhere. Dad went to bring in the meat. The Bombardier traveled across the ice, up along side the caribou. The bombardier had 2 seats, Dad driving and his Helper in the second seat. I was in the back. Dad shot 3 caribou and put them in the back with Mike and I. We were somehow on the Caribou, between their legs. Somehow one of the caribous moved. You heard some screaming, both Mike and I wanted, scrambled out of the back, but there was no space for us to scramble any where. We believed the Caribou was still alive. we were yelling and screaming.

The Stark Lake camp consisted of The Mine Manager, Dave & Madeline Ardle, his wife was the camp cook for the Miners. There were 4 Miners. Dad and a helper. My mom, 4-year-old brother Mike & our baby sister Hazel. The Ardle's had a dog and we had our dog, Buddy.

By Christmas a third one room cabin had been built. It was built for the mine office but, Art Ridley the senior of the brothers told Dad we could move into this.

I loved this cabin, not like the cabins I had experienced to this point, in my life. It was one big room with higher ceiling and windows looking out onto Stark lake. I was accustomed to cabins made of logs and to insulate covered with mud. There was a small sawmill at the mining camp. The cabins were built of boards, clean cut, fresh smelling boards. The inside walls were boards. The outside walls, also these boards. The space between the inside and outside walls filled with sawdust for insulation. We were no longer cold. With this insulation, the wood stove on during the day, kept the cabin, comparatively warm for most of the night.

Often Caribou would be out on Stark Lake. The caribou liked being on the lake, they could see the wolves coming from some distance. Looking through our window, was a beautiful sight.

Like every winter, this winter, again our winter diet was caribou. When needed, it was easier to hunt caribou with the bombardier than with a dog team. Dad saw a herd of caribou out on the lake. Our meat supply was low. Dad jumped into the two-seat bombardier, Dad helper into the second seat, Mike and I wanted to go too. Dad said jump in, stand behind the seats. Like this we were soon across the lake in amongst the caribou. Dad shot 3 and put them in the back with Mike and I. Mike and I sitting on the caribou. A short time later, one of the caribous moved. This had Mike and I, yelling and screaming, scrambling for the front, but there was no room, in the front. Dad said "settle down it, that was only a late muscle twitch" Mike and I were not totally convinced but there was little we could do. Somehow, driving through the herd of Buffalo, years later, Dad screaming, "turn around, let's get out of this buffalo herd and spend the night in the village of Providence" Somehow, recalled how scared Mike and I were, the time I was sitting on the Caribou. Sweet revenge? No, only a coincidence? I have no idea why this incident flashed through my head, those many years later, the night scared my father driving through the Buffalo herd.

CHAPTER 7

FREIGHTING ACROSS GREAT SLAVE LAKE

The bombardier would pull a sleigh, a sleigh similar to a flat bed trailer a five-ton truck would pull down the highway. This sleigh would carry, laying on their side, a plie of about 15, 45-gallon drums of gasoline across the ice of Great Slave Lake from Yellowknife to the Mine, Stark Lake.

The empty drums, to return would be, on their side, piled high on the sleigh. On their side there would be a small tunnel, between each drum, in which a boy age 4 could crawl.

Mike said to me, one day, "you know how we could go to Yellowknife with Dad?" All we have to do is crawl in between the drums. I was thinking Mike was joking, No! this is exactly what he did. When he did, he kept it a secret, even from me.

Dad left. Some time after mom noticed Mike missing. Everyone in camp started a frantic search. After some time mom guessed "could he have been in the bombardier" Art Ridley was in camp, with his small bush airplane that day. Art flew the distance to the bombardier. Landed. Dad stopped, wondering what is wrong. Mike, very cold crawled out from between the drums. The empty barrels, bouncing as the sleigh went over each snow drift, scared Mike, but did not crush him.

Perhaps at that time, Mom, Dad realized with Mike's adventuresome spirit, uncontrollable quest for adventure, his life would be a short one.

...Over the years I had felt my Dad's big hands across my bottom, on many, many, occasions. Usually when my brother and I would fight. Seems to me, Mike would normally start it. Me being two years older, I had the advantage, hence he would after a moment, run, tell Dad. Whoever told Dad first, the other was in trouble. Mike normally told dad first, hence Dad's big hand would make a firm impact with my bottom. My dad was a loving dad, mom loved us, we 4 children knew our parents loved us very much, we were poor, but we were loved.

That spring the mining camp closed down and we returned to Yellowknife. The Ridley brothers did not pay their employees and we were very broke.

CHAPTER 8

VIC & GABRIEL DUMONT

We moved into a three, room shack, outdoor toilet, no running water, the occasional bath was when mom heated a tub of water on the wood stove. I must have smelt, I know I smelt, smelt bad.

There were 3 rooms in this little house. One half was the living room, going through an open door, took you into the kitchen, one quarter of the house, a second open doorway into mom and dad's bedroom. There were no doors on the doorway, there would not have been space for the doors to swing open and closed.

Enter Vic Dumont: Our house was so very small, there was no room for us children to sleep. Vic said to mom, I will open the ceiling at the end of the living room, and build a narrow stairway for the children to sleep in the attic.

Vic Dumont, visited often, mom would invite him for lunch, whatever we had. Vic was a generation older than mom and dad, yet enjoyed their company, was a good friend.

Vic's grandfather was Gabriel Dumont. Mom would sometime leave Vic to babysit us. One of these was, the week my mother was in the hospital for the birth of my youngest sister Linda. Vic would tell us the stories, his grandfather told him. These stories scared me and at the same time fascinated me. I was 7 at the time, the Korean War was on the news every evening. A combination of Vic's stories and the voice, words of the news announcer, I could not sleep at nights. The wars on the Canadian Prairies, are not the subject of movies, as they are in the United States, yet Vic, told them well, in graphic detail, as any movie.

There were so many similarities, seemed like our north made no progress, during these three generations, Gabriel Dumont, could not read, not write. Neither mom, nor Vic, could read nor write. Mom did not go to school, not one day in her life. Mom laments, the Residential Schools had not made their way into the North West Territories, yet during her youth. Mom went through life frustrated, that these schools were not in the north. Those that did attend these schools, are able to read and write, some have, have used this knowledge to achieve. Some have found a way, to have John A. Macdonald's statue torn off their foundation's, have found a way to have governments write checks.

As a student of Canadian events, World events, why do those that were able to attend Residential Schools, continually criticize the results and those before the Residential Schools, be so envious of those who were able to attend Residential Schools. I am totally confused by the differences. I know my mother would have "given her right arm" for an education.

One has to digress, explain Gabriel Dumont. **Gabriel Dumont (December 1837-May 1906) was a Canadian political figure best known for being a prominent leader of the <u>Métis</u> people. Dumont was well known for his movements within the <u>North-West Rebellion</u> at the Battles of <u>Batoche</u>, <u>Fish Creek</u>, and <u>Duck Lake</u> as well as for his role in the signing of treaties with the Blackfoot tribe, the traditional main enemy of the Métis.**

Dumont was born to Isidore Dumont and Louise Laframboise in 1837 in Red River. Growing up Dumont had little in the way of education – he was illiterate but could speak seven languages. [1] In the early stages of his life, Dumont relied on buffalo hunting in order to gain a source of food. His family made a living through hunting buffalo and trading with the Hudson's Bay Company. After his time leading the Métis people alongside Louis Riel, Dumont spent time travelling throughout the United States where he spoke at public speaking events and political campaigns. In 1889 he dictated his memoirs in Quebec.

Dumont known throughout the Métis community for his various political and military endeavours. Among his chiefest political campaigns was the severing of a treaty between the Métis and the Dakota in 1882. Just one year later, Dumont was elected hunt chief of the Saskatchewan Métis. Dumont was known as the adjutant general of the Métis people – he played a large role in the well-being of the Métis community and their subsequent resistance against the Canadian government during the North-West Rebellion. Dumont also figured prominently in the Duck Lake conflict, as well as the battles of Fish Creek and Batoche

Vic Dumont: Our house was so very small, there was no room for us children to sleep. Vic said to mom, I will open the ceiling at the end of the living room, and build a narrow stairway for the children to sleep in the attic. With the steep pitch of the roof, the center of the attic was over 6 feet high. Vic made a place for my two sisters and a cousin, the 3 to sleep in one bed, at one end of the attic. A partial wall, with open door, separated us. My brother and I slept at the other end. Vic installed windows which could be opened at both ends of the attic. He nailed a 2" X 4" ladder on the outside of the house, so we could get out, in case of a fire. From this window, we could get out at night. This came in handy during the gardens, harvest season. We could get out while our parents were sleeping and go raid gardens.

We could also climb out from the window on our end. My brother and I could climb out put this only put us on top the front porch. I recall, one sunny summer day, I was sitting on top the porch with a very full bucket of water in my hands. Uncle Danny and Aunt Doris, lived and an even smaller house next door. They spent most of their leisure time at our house. With a huge smile on my face, I was waiting for one of them to come out the front door.

CHAPTER 9

REVENGE ON THE PRACTICAL JOKER

Uncle Danny, always happy, did like to tease. He had earlier, given me a cheap shot, teased me about something, possibly it was kissing the rabbits butt again, or something similar. A young man can always be teased about girls. Anyway, here I was sitting on top of the roof of the porch. My feet, legs, straddling the peak. Dad, saw me. He thought he was going to "fix me." With an even bigger smile on his face, all of a sudden, the biggest bucket of water, came over my head and all down my back. I was soaked. Dad was laughing. He had snuck up behind me and through the oven window, drenched me. What could I say? I had to laugh. The roles had reversed. I was waiting for Uncle Danny or Auntie Doris, instead it was me, who was soaking wet. We were poor, but we had good times. This house was our house. Uncle Danny was mom's youngest brother.

Nobody had told me at the time, but Auntie Doris was also my half sister, from my father's side. A daughter Dad had while he was still a teenager from a previous relationship. Auntie Doris had been raised by her mother and step father, so initially, I had no way of knowing. Doris, looked so very much like, dad, like the 4 of us, mom's children, I began asking questions. As was often the case, small nothing communities, we were related through two lines.

Because my sister was raised by her mother, she was able to get her full native status. She was privy to some of the benefits, later in life, a free house.

There was no running water, in our home. During the winter a water truck would come to our house and fill up a 45gallon drum we had sitting in the kitchen, hence no indoor flushing toilet.

After a few years of going outside at minus 40 degrees, my mother decided we needed something indoors. We were getting tired of sitting on a freezing board. Sitting on my bidet today, warm water shooting on my butt, I sometimes think about those 40 degrees below zero boards.

CHAPTER 10

THE HONEY WAGON

Yellowknife was divided into the "old town" and up the hill, the "new town." The new town had regular, as we all have today, water pipes, sewer pipes into their homes.

Some of the "classier" people in the "old town", had an indoor toilet, which basically consisted of a bucket inside a bigger bucket. The bigger bucket had regular toilet seats and an exhaust pipe, out through the roof, which theoretically was to allow the smells to escape. Mom decided we were going to buy one of these. Mom asked Vic, to make a small room, big enough to sit down. Make this room at the foot of my bed. Vic did so, and installed the toilet. Dad mostly being away, on the boat in the summer, Arctic Ice Roads in the winter, being the oldest, it was my job to empty the inner bucket, before it got full. There were times, I wished I had done it sooner. To many times, it was a job I hated and at times neglected until it was to late. It had to be dumped into about a 15-gallon drum outside at the road, the city had hired Ted Cinnamon, (the older brother of the sawmill owner) to haul away the 45-gallon drums of regular garbage and Ted, had another truck with a tank on the back, into which he dumped these 15-gallon drums.

Those times that I procrastinated dumping the inner bucket from our attic toilet, the inner drum would overflow and start to fill up the outer bucket. This overflowing bucket, still with that, which was clinging to the outside, from the outer bucket, now had to be carried through the room of my brother and I, through my sister's room, down the narrow steps, through the living room, out to the drum at the road. Now I had to go back and wipe up the floor, anyplace, I had splashed, the droppings. After that I would go through a period of time, when I would dump the inner bucket before it was completely full, but invariably there were times, I would procrastinate again. Ted Cinnamon would be coming up the road, he would see me rushing to dump my bucket, before he left. I do not know who had the dirtier job, me or Ted Cinnamon. I guess to hide our situation from ourselves, we gave these un comfortable situations names. The bucket, was called the "honey bucket". Ted Cinnamon's sewage truck was called the "honey wagon". The conversation would go like this.

When mom had to leave the house early, she would say to me "the honey wagon goes by today, be sure you get the honey bucket to the road before the honey wagon goes by."

I did not like the job, I would procrastinate to the last minute, as I saw the "honey wagon" coming down the street, Ted Cimmamon would see me. The honey bucket was heavy, all I could handle, struggling, not to splash myself, sometimes I was successful, getting the "honey bucket" to the road on time.

Last week, I was at the road, when our North Vancouver garbage men came by. He gave me "shit" because I failed to wash the empty ketchup bottle before putting it in the blue bin.

The year we returned from Stark Lake, September, I was 7, almost 8 years old. I was, at last to start school, seriously. I was now 2 years behind those students, my classmates of the few months we were in Yellowknife, when I was 6, when we first came from Rocher river. I clearly remember, In the school yard, the prettiest girl, laughing, talking to her friend, "that boy was with me in grade one, and he is till in grade 1." Being behind the others, not having regular baths, I guess this is what gave the older students permission to beat me up.

The native kids would beat me up because they thought I was white. The white kids would beat me up because they thought I was native. In particular, I remember 2 brothers who liked beating me. Each end of school day, there were 3 buses waiting to return school kids home. My bus was the first one, take us to the old town of Yellowknife. A second bus for con Mine children and a third bus for the Giant Mine children.

I would wait and wait to exit the school doors and run for the bus, hoping to get there before the brothers caught me. Most often I failed, they had me down on the ground beating, me. As I had to catch the first bus, and they the third bus, there were days they could cause me to miss my bus and still catch their bus. I would walk, the distance home.

By now we were in grade 3. I was tired of the near daily beating. I burst out the school door and instead of running for the bus, I ran towards the brother on my right. The surprize to him and even more to me, I knocked him over, he started running in the other direction. I then ran at the brother to my left and he ran in the other direction. Wow! why had I not done this the year earlier. That may have been the last time, I let someone beat on me. To this day, people get a quick reaction. Like everyone I have worked for some Bosses, who were bullies, but I respond quickly, this, not always to my benefit. Honest, have to admit, there were times, I wish, I had been more diplomatic.

By the time I was nine, Dad had given up hunting/ trapping and made or living operating heavy equipment. Uncle Danny and Uncle Ray were still hunting/ Trapping. Each spring, my uncles, Uncle Ray and Uncle Danny would come to Yellowknife for the festivities, the celebrations, the Canadian Championship Dog Derby, Yellowknife 50mile Dog team races. Over the years my Uncle Ray won the race many times and Uncle Danny won the race, even more.

CHAPTER 11

RETURNING FOR GRANDMA'S RHUBARB PIE

That same year, the year I was nine, during school break, March, Uncle Danny was returning to Rocher River after winning the race. I decided to visit my grandmother, mom's mother, owned a small restaurant in the village of about 100 people. I remembered, she baked the best rhubarb/ apple pies. She grew the rhubarb in her garden. I do not know where she got the apple, the cinnamon.

Early that morning, early, I crawled into the 3-star eiderdown sleeping bag, that every dog musher carried in their toboggan, to keep warm. My uncle, would mush the dogs from here, if I was not in the sleeping bag. "Mush", said my uncle, the dogs were off, running, they loved to run, loved to pull. Tails flying in the air. The distance across Great Slave Lake is approximately 100 miles, a 2-day trip. Today my uncle stood on the back, holding onto the "backboard". My uncle said "If we can reach Outpost Island before dark, some hunters are living in a cabin there. We can sleep inside, instead of sleeping outside in the snow.

When the Trappers use a camp for only one night, sleeping outside in the snow is very rudimentary. When the dogs stop, each dog is taken from the harness and chained to neighboring trees. Second about 5 full length trees are knocked down, into a plie and lite on fire, this will burn all night. Snow is kicked from an area big enough for a sleeping bag, near the fire. Spruce boroughs, branches, are cut from other trees and woven into a bed, to insulate the canvas/ sleeping bag from the frozen ground. The sheet canvas, twice or three times the size of the sleeping bag, big enough to go under and around on top of the sleeping bag. The trapper crawls into the sleeping bag and pulls the canvas up over, covers his head.

We arrived at the cabins, at outpost Island, as darkness was arriving. We had made it, we did not need to sleep outside. We knocked on the door, and were invited in. Dinner was on the stove. The March spring hunt, trappers are looking to catch, for the furs of beaver and muskrats. This is what they eat. There was a pot full of muskrat carcases boiling on the stove. We were invited to join them for dinner. I had eaten muskrat, when I was younger, when Dad was still a trapper. After mushing dogs all day to arrive here, I was very hungry. Those muskrats tasted so good. I have never eaten, muskrats since. I could not handle it today. How spoiled have I become?

The following day, we arrived in Rocher River. My grandmother's rhubarb pie was so much better. My grandmother's rhubarb pies, were always great, but after eating muskrats the night before, it was worth travelling this distance for these pies.

Rocher River, was a village of about 100 people. On one end was my mother's mother, my grandmother's restaurant. On the other end of village was the other side, my Dad's dad, my grandfather, was in competition with Hudson's Bay Company, had a small fur trading store. My grandfather also had 4 horses. I rode these horses every day, ate my grandmother's rhubarb pie, every day, for the 10 days of Easter Holiday break. My grandfather, had timed a business trip to Yellowknife, to coincide with my need to return to Yellowknife for end of spring break. He had chartered a bush airplane Cessna 180, to fly us to Yellowknife. Once in the air the pilot let me take the controls, hold the controls on the passenger's side. A very memorable ten days for a young man of nine.

CHAPTER 12

HOW DO I MAKE SOME MONEY?

I wanted to make money, help my parents. What could I do? Some of the students were selling the local Newspaper. "News of the North" I was now making some friends, I was getting some confidence. Mark Horton, a friend's family owned the newspaper. I found I loved selling. Selling the news was easy. People liked me, they were always ready with their dime, when I knocked on their door. My Parents said, "Len, the money is yours, start a bank account." Next, I started selling the Star Weekly, my bank account grew.

We always kept a team of huskies. We always had dogs in our back yard. During winter months, those days that I was not selling my newspapers, I was visiting my fur traps. I would hitch 2 or 3 dogs and mush along the shore of Great Slave Lake until I passed the Yellowknife Con Mine. My parents had taught me how to set traps and skin fur. I set traps for wolves and foxes, mostly foxes. I have to be honest, this was emotionally difficult. The most difficult when I came upon a trap where the fox was alive. I would have to club it over the head, to kill it. We were Trappers. I came from a family of Trappers, we had to earn a living. Selling the pelts, this helped my bank account grow. In the spring of the year, I would trap muskrats and beaver.

I would also hunt. On the weekends I would leave the house early, Go beyond Con mine, or across the ice of Yellowknife Bay, to the area of Burwash and hunt ptarmigan. I would also hunt beyond Con Mine, to the south of Yellowknife, sometimes north beyond Giant Mine. I normally avoided the streets of Yellowknife, but one day I was hunting, where it was shorter to walk home, through the streets.

The Police, RCMP, stopped me. "What are you doing?"

"I am hunting ptarmigan", I proudly held up my 3ptarmigan.

He said "Get in the car"

I answered "No, its not necessary, I am almost home"

"Get in the car!" came the answer.

He drove me the rest of the way home, knocked on the door and entered our shack.

He said to my mother, "I caught your son, hunting Ptarmigan"

My mother was puzzled, she was thinking, so what? She answered "Yes, we are licenced hunters, trappers."

Police "but he has a gun."

Again, my mother said "Yes, we are licenced hunters, trappers."

This went back and forth, each communicating past the other. Me wondering what is the problem?

Police, "but he is 10 years old."

Mother, "yes, he was hunting Ptarmigan for dinner"

Then the police said "he has to be 14 to carry a gun"

My mother said "ok, he will never hunt again." The police left.

My mother turned and said to me "Never, walk back on the streets of Yellowknife, hunt in the areas, where this this is not necessary"

I, selling newspapers, trapping furs, I soon had a thousand dollars in the bank. I was preparing for University. Dad often told me, "Len, I will never be able to afford to pay for your University. Drive truck for Curry Construction and play hockey for the Yellowknife Indians." But I was saving, a thousand dollars was lot of money in those days. Yellowknife had less than 3,000 people, but from the community at Giant Mine on one side to the community at Con Mine, on the other side of Yellowknife, spread over a great distance. I walked it, sometimes drove my dogs. Knocked on every door, sold as many newspapers as possible. Everybody in town knew me. I was getting a reputation as a workaholic. When I turned 14, Bruce Weaver offered me a real job. Weaver & Devore's store offered me a job, stocking shelves after school and Saturdays. My bank account grew. As I got older I received more job offers.

At 16 I received the job offer that was to shape my life. At 7 years old, I was walking the streets of Yellowknife. With both my hands folded, in my pockets, a little hungry, I thought, said quietly under my breath "who has the money in this town?" Norman W. Byrne. "What does he do?" "I need to meet him, work for him, someday"

My opportunity came about when, a friend Danny Pappas, went to Norm Byrne and asked for a summer job. But at that moment, Norman W. Byrne Ltd. / Precambrian Mining services ltd, had not yet decided to hire a summer student.

Danny Pappas decided to spend his summer in Edmonton. A few days later, they were ready to hire a summer student. Shorty Brown, informed George Pappas, Danny's father, Yes, they were ready to hire Danny. George said "Danny is in Edmonton, but the hardest working young man, Leonard De Melt, has his driver's license and would possibly love the job. I was born in Con Mine, first aid shack, and now at 16, I had my first job, for a mining company. "I was on a roll." Later Danny told me, "that was my job, had my father told me they were ready to hire me, I would have returned to Yellowknife." I will be forever indebted to Danny. I was on my way, I was working for Norman w. Byrne. Yet, only later did I realize the complete importance of this.

During these earlier years I trapped furs and delivered Newspapers, during the winter months. The summers go not last long in the near arctic, but still, we do have summers. Long summer days. The 21 st. of June there is 24 hours of bright daylight. Of course, the newspapers continued during the summers of age 8 to 14, but these were weekly newspapers. I, Mike and I had a lot of spare time, during summer holidays. How could we have some fun and earn some money.

CHAPTER 13

THE SECOND BOAT, SANDY JEAN.

By the time, I was 8 years old, Dad had traded in his very small boat for one, just a little bigger. A boat called "Sandy Jean". Dad and Uncle Danny made up the two man crew. This boat, depending on the weather, pushed or pulled a barge. This barge could haul a load of lumber or mining camp supplies. Glen Cinnamon, owned a saw mill on the south side of Great Slave Lake, up the Slave River. Yellowknife is on the North side of Great Slave lake, hence it was Dad's and our boats job to get the lumber from the sawmill, to the mining town of Yellowknife. We near lost our lives but, we learned boating, to swim, fishing, we had a lot of fun on that boat during those summers.

The Slave River is a very sandy river, one can not see a foot of the depth. The sand forms a number of sand bars, one being in the form of a horseshoe. This made the water relatively still and a great place to swim, while the boat was tied up at the dock, waiting for the loading of the barge. My uncle Danny, (Danny McQueen) enjoyed swimming with us. He would take my brother and I along with the Cinnamon children to the Horseshoe sandbar. With the Arctic's short summers, us children did not have much opportunity to learn to swim. We would float on the life jackets, we had taken from the boat. This was our opportunity to take a proper bath.

One of these occasions, I, peacefully floating on one of the life jackets. I had it under me, more in the form of a chair, than placed properly about my body.

Uncle Danny pulled the life jacket out from under me.

The hysteria!

Uncle Danny, Don't, don't I yelled and sputtered, sandy water filling my mouth and nose, "but wait" I splashed about! Suddenly, I found myself swimming.

"Look, look, Uncle Danny" I said "I can swim, do not give me the life jacket back. Luckily, I was near the sand bar, a few strokes and I climbed out.

I never did become a good swimmer, but I can swim well enough to today, have fun with my children. They, being mostly raised in the south, swim like fish.

I had my share of close calls and wonder why I am still alive but my brother. Everyone who knew Mike, knew he would never live to a "rip old age"

On the Sandy Jean, those summers, Mike first encounter with death was during a storm. The waves on Great Slave Lake can reach, 10 to 15 feet high. When these storms start to blow up the Sandy Jean must head for harbor. About 50 miles across, in the center, there is an island called "OutPost Island" To see over the barge when the boat was pushing a load of lumber, the steering wheel, control cabin stood 10 feet above the main cabin on the boat. On this occasion, half way through the trip, the blustery wind, vicious wind began to howl, seemed the control cabin on top the boat, near touched the water, first to the left and then to the right, rocking back and forth.

Dad turned in the direction of Outpost Island to wait out the storm. Mike decided to "kill time" by taking out a fishing rod. Standing on the slippery, wet rocks, as the waves crashed on shore, Mike slid down the slope into the water, between the Sandy Jean and the mooring. Uncle Danny saw him, threw Mike a line, a small rope, and somehow got Mike out of harms way before the next wave drove the boat into the mooring.

That was not the end of Mike challenging the elements that summer. The Slave River carries huge amounts of sand, building up sandbars below the surface of the water. Dad knew the river very well, but sand shifts, and builds up. Those sand bars that were lower in the water, sometimes grew. Dad leaving the sawmill going down river, found the Sandy Jean, come to a sudden and abrupt stop. They were firmly lodged on a sand bar. "Anybody have any ideas?" Dad had one canoe with a 10 horsepower, outboard motor. There was a second person with a similar canoe, in a cabin near the mouth of the river. "let's get him to help."

They hooked a line from the Sandy Jean to Dad's canoe, Uncle Danny running the motor. A second line running from this middle canoe to the second canoe in front. "OK, rev the outboard motors to the maximum and pull."

This did not work, the way the ropes, were tied the canoe in the middle with my by now, 7 year old brother, Mike and Uncle Danny flipped. The Slave River runs with a great deal of force. This volume of water moves swiftly. By some miracle, Mike bobbed up on one side to the overturned canoe, with Uncle Danny surfacing on the opposite side. Reaching over the canoe, Uncle Danny was able to grab Mike. The river swirling by, tugging at their waist, tugging at their legs. Mike says to Uncle Danny "hold me, hold me, I am slipping. The front canoe was fighting against the current to get turned around. To pick Uncle Danny and Mike from the water.

The turn was successful. My brother and uncle were saved. Did Mike learn? Seems, Mike continued to challenge the elements at each opportunity.

The last trip. These summers, aboard Sandy Jean came to an end the year I was 12 years old. The fall of the year. The ice was beginning to form on Great Slave Lake. The days were getting very short, the nights very long, very dark.

Glen Cinnamon wanted one trip. Glen needed the money, one more barge load of lumber in Yellowknife. Glen wanted one more trip.

Dad said "No!" "Please, no Glen, the ice is forming on the lake." "There is almost a 100% chance the ice will form, freeze the Sandy Jean in the middle of Great Slave Lake, fore the winter. If frozen in the shifting ice, the wooden hull, of the Sandy Jean will be crushed."

Dad had traded his little boat. Glen had put up the balance of the money to buy the boat, hence had the authority.

Glen said "Ok, If, you will not Captain the boat, for one more trip, this fall, I will Captain the boat.

Dad got on a bush plane to fly back to Yellowknife.

Glen started out across Great Slave Lake for the final trip that summer and as it turned out, for the final trip ever. For fear of the forming ice, Glen carried on during the dark night, load of lumber, steaming towards Yellowknife. Glen did not, not see a reef in the water. The barge slammed into the reef blew apart, looked like wood kindling. The last load of lumber was floating everywhere. The loss of this load of lumber, put Glen under. Without these dollars, he could not carry on the following year. This was the end.

I overheard Dad talking to Uncle Danny. "Well, that was not so bad, those years were not so bad." "I did get my house paid for." I thought "This three, room shack. It seemed to me, this could be built in a little over a week, a month at most. We over these years, got all our groceries at Weaver & Devore, Bruce Weaver's store. It was more expensive than the other stores in town, but Dad said "this was ok, Bruce never asked to be paid." Bruce would let Dad pay him, whenever Dad had some money. Bruce waited a very long time for his money that fall.

During those summers, Mike and I did not spend all our time on the Sandy Jean. Sometimes we would take turns travelling with dad. Sometimes we would both stay in town. Of course, the newspapers continued during the summers of age 8 to 14, but these were weekly newspapers. I, Mike and I had a lot of spare time, during summer holidays. How could we have some fun and earn some money.

CHAPTER 14

RAFTING ACROSS, GREAT SLAVE LAKE'S. YELLOWKNIFE BAY

Initially we made rafts, to cross the waters of Yellowknife Bay. We paddled all over Yellowknife Bay. We set fish nets.

There was a lumber yard, Johnson's lumber yard a short distance from our house. The 2" X 12" X 20 foot lumber was right on the very edge, of the dock. If the lumber flipped over it would land in the water. 6 of these Boards nailed together would make a great raft. We my brother and I, sometimes with a neighbor, Jay Forrest, assemble these rafts. Sometimes we would often have 3 or 4 of these rafts tied up where the path from our house meet the lake. We would go up and down the neighborhood, selling these fish for 25 cents each. My university account was growing.

Jay Forrest was the third oldest of four brothers. Tommy, the oldest, and Bobby, second oldest were half a generation older than us, Jay was the age of us, one year younger than me, one year older than, my brother Mike. Mickey was the youngest of the Forrest clan. About five years younger than Jay, but still tagged along, so you would see the four of us together. Myself. Jay, Mike and Mickey.

Rumor had it that the older two brothers Tommy and Bobby, were sent away to Reform School, for disciplinary action, to the outside world, anything south of North West territories was considered the "Outside World"

Mary Forrest, their mother, enjoyed a drink, she always had a barrel of moonshine going in their back room. Jay would take me to it, take the cover off and ask me if I wanted to try some. I always said "I will try it later, when it is more fermented, the fruit, vegetables or whatever it was made of, floating around on top of the concoction, turned me off." I did try one, once it was bottled. I do not know how anyone could drink that.

On of the locations, Mary enjoyed "throwing back a few drinks" was at the home of Archie Loutitte. Mrs. Forrest (Mary) was friends with Mr. And Mrs. Loutitte (Archie). Jay would sometimes be at his mother's side. Archie's house was between our house and the water. Archie's back yard was the water, Yellowknife Bay, Great Slave lake. Jay returned from Archie's one day, quoting Archie, "Timbers, the size a grown man could not handle, float up along my yard here, and yet the De Melt kids handle them. Archie did not know we threw them off the top of the pile of lumber in Johnson's lumber yard. The lumber yard immediately against the water, along the shore to the north of our home. One flip, Turning the boards over, we could get them to land in the water. Somehow, we rationalized that our dad's boat hauled these from Cinnamon's sawmill. This was not theft. We had access to a few boards. I expect, if Ivar Johnson knew what we were doing, he would have a different opinion.

Hunting in the winter, net fishing in the summer. As we grew a little older, Chippi Loctite had a skiff he was not using, dad had an older model 10 horsepower outboard motor, the became ours, Mike and I. we were able to replace our rafts. We were able to fish, greater distances from home. We were able to fish the Yellowknife River rapids.

This was great fun, we would arrive at Yellowknife Rapids and set gill nets. The fish would pool at the bottom of the Rapids. Within a short time, few hours, we would have 10 to 20 fish. With 24hour daylight, this one evening we arrived at the Rapids about 8:00pm. Set our nets, by 1:00 am, we were tired, pulled our nets, put our fish on the shore and crawled into our sleeping bags, fell soundly to sleep, obviously very soundly to sleep. The sound of water rushing over the Rapids was soothing to the ears. When we four, woke up in the morning all our fish were gone. I was certain a bear, had come during the night and ate all our fish.

When I arrived home, I told mom "a bear came and stole all our catch, we had to stay longer to catch more."

Mom said "No, it had to be people."

I said "We would have heard people, the noise of the outboard motor"

The people from north of the Rapids, the four families at Bluefish falls, had constructed a system of rails and pulleys to portage their boats, along the shore, parallel to the Rapids. This allowed them to get from Bluefish falls to Yellowknife during summer months.

Mom said "these people must have gone by during the night" I was convinced we would have heard them; the noise of the rapids could have drowned out the outboard motor noise?

I still believed it was a bear. Who stole our fish? Could mom be right? Mom is pretty smart.

CHAPTER 15

TOMMY IS DEAD

Winter came, Bobby Forrest was now a young adult, had returned to Yellowknife, became a Diamond Driller, which meant he spent most of his time in "the bush" on drilling jobs. Bobby had bought a car. This car was parked in the Forrest's yard.

Jay came to me "Len, mom is sleeping, lets quietly push the car out of the yard and practice driving."

I said "No, the police, brought me home, when I walked through town with a gun, they will surely catch us, if we start driving."

Jay said "we will immediately get on the ice roads, lets go"

In the winter Yellowknife Bay freezes with about 6feet of ice. The plough trucks doze roads across the ice, to haul freight to the Mines and Communities further north. Where possible, they would sometimes plough the roads out to the width of a small airport. These widths would last longer, take longer to fill in from blowing, drifting snow. The wider the road, the longer the time, before the plough truck would need to return to plough the roads again.

We did exactly as Jay said. Checked to see Mrs. Forrest was sleeping soundly, helped that she enjoyed, "throwing back a few drinks". She was sleeping. Let's go, quickly and quietly, we often, pushed the car out of the yard.

Drive onto the ice, behind our homes, we would take turns driving. Slippery ice, we would drive as fast as we could, step on the brakes and put the car into a spin, wow this was "a ball"

Were the ice roads where narrower, we would take turns driving, the game was, we would go faster and faster, until we hit the snowbank on the side of the road. We would then dig ourselves out, and now it was the other persons turn to drive until we hit the snowbank again. Back and forth, taking turns.

Tommy Forrest, the oldest brother, adult as we were in our young teens, returned to Yellowknife, only during the summers. Tommy Forrest was a great baseball player. The NHL hockey league was only six teams at the time. The young men, who did not make, or had not yet made, the international baseball and hockey teams, worked in the mines. The mines scouted these fellows, offering them jobs. Each of Canada's mines wanted the best hockey / baseball teams. Yellowknife mines included, wanted the best possible teams.

Tommy Forrest was the best of these baseball players. Tommy Forrest had no idea who I was, the younger playmates of his brother, but I knew who he was.

It seems that near 50% of the young men of Yellowknife, between guns and bush airplanes, meet a young death. One day I was walking in front of the Yellowknife Hotel. With two buddies, each side of him, Tommy Forrest was walking 10feet in front. Something had gone wrong at baseball. Tommy was upset with a coach, or umpires call. I overheard Tommy's buddy say "well. It's not like you are going to die tomorrow."

About a week later, Jay knocked on our door. Early in the morning. Jay was crying. It was impossible to make Jay cry, we would wrestle, I was year older, makes a big difference at this age. I could not get him to say "Uncle". Regardless of the pressure I put on him, he was in pain, he would not concede. Why was he crying this morning?

I opened the door. "Jay, why are your crying?"

Jay responded "Tommy"

"What?", I asked

"Tommy is dead, Tommy got shot."

"What?" "How?" "What happened?"

Tommy had gone to Yellowknife Rapids, climbed out of the canoe. The shotgun was still in the canoe. Tommy reached back to pull the shotgun out of the canoe, the barrel was pointing at him, the trigger got stuck as he was pulling it. The gun went off, the bullet hitting Tommy.

CHAPTER 16

BUILDING WINTER ICE ROADS.

These years, Dad's summer job was the Sandy Jean. During the winters Dad built Arctic Ice roads, the forerunner of today's Arctic Ice Roads. The North West Territories is a network of Lakes. There are lakes everywhere. The majority of Territories is only some minor distance above sea level. The frozen north does not have the climate for evaporation. Flying across the Arctic in a bush plane, newcomers to the north are surprised, lakes everywhere. By joining the lakes with land portages, between the lakes, ice roads can be made, predominantly over lakes to the isolated Mines and Communities of the Northwest Territories. The town of Yellowknife was not joined to the roads in the south until the year I was 14. The Mackenzie highway was finished in 1960. A rough gravel highway but this year we were connected to the South. Prior to this, Boat pushing barges, hauled supplies to Yellowknife in the summer. Airplanes and Caterpillar Trains in the winter.

The dangers of building these winter ice roads were numerous. The science and understanding of Ice Roads had not progressed until many years later. Initially, where to travel on the ice, areas of bad ice, areas to stay away from was mostly a "gut Feeling". Dan had spent his whole life on ice, first with dog teams, then with Bombardiers, next Caterpillar Tractors and later Trucks. Jack Perkins owned 6, D4 Caterpillar Tractors. Dad would run the lead tractor, it was his job, in addition to run the lead tractor, avoid bad ice. His job to spot the pressure ridges before the tractor dropped through the ice, a few hundred feet and fell to the bottom of the lake.

"Pressure Ridges" Ice expands as it freezes. The surface, the area, the ice wants to occupy is a much larger area than the surface of the lake. Depending on the shape of the lake, the depth of the lake, there are weaker and stronger blocks, locations across the lake. At the weaker areas the ice crushes and pushes up forming a ridge of open water full of ice cubes. These areas of open water are not always easy to see when covered with snow.

On different occasions, Dad jumped from the machine to avoid going down with the machine. Landing on the broken ice, ice cubes and scrambling, Dad was able to save his life these times.

Another of the dangers, the owners always used the oldest of their equipment in the arctic. When the equipment was to old to work on the highways in the South, the Owners would send the machines North.

Those years there were 2 mines further into the North. The Discovery Mine and the Tundra Mine. As often as I could, around my school work, my jobs, I would travel with Dad. I wanted to learn. If I could not earn enough money to go to University, I would need to be doing this.

On this occasion, my newspapers were delivered for the week, it was Easter, school break. Dad was driving an old Mack truck, hauling a lot to the Discovery Mine. They had been loading the trailer during the day, Dad was to leave in the evening. Dad asked if I wanted to go along. I was always excited about making these trips with dad. The summer trips, the winter trips, the bush planes with dad's friends, when I could, I never missed an opportunity.

"Yes. Of course, I want to go along"

We walked across the yard from our house to dad's employer, Byer's Transport yard. Dad walked around the truck, inspecting it. It did not look good, The exhaust piping under the truck this looked especially bad. Dad had tools, also Byers employed a mechanic. Anxious to get going, some temporary repairs were made. This was a mistake, Temporary repairs for these Arctic Ice roads.

The distance over lakes was relatively smooth but the portages between the lakes are rough, very rough, often swamp land in the summer, muskeg, this freezes unevenly with big holes, holes big enough for the complete wheel to drop into, makes the bumpiest, most dangerous, slowest ride, one can imagine. Try to go a little faster? The result is a broken axle.

We set out driving across Yellowknife Bay, the first portages were rough but ok. With the winters 20-hour nights, we were now well into the middle of the night. The fourth portage, right front wheel dropped into the hole. Twisted the axle, the total, surprising the steel frames can take this amount of twisting. The wheel spun and climbed out of this hole. At 49 degrees below zero, the steel becomes so very crystalized, steel snaps, breaks like glass. We thought ok, close but we are still, ok.

Then exhaust fumes started to enter the cab. Dad stuck rags in the holes in the floor. We were getting gassed. Severely gassed, 49 degrees below zero, we opened all the windows, tried to stick our heads out the window, but the grinding, howling engine, looking for more horsepower, to pull us out of the continues potholes, the road in the frozen muskeg was one continues pothole, continues potholes. The exhaust fumes were boiling out from under the truck, through the floor and up around the out side of the truck. We looked like a moving ball of exhaust gas, inside and outside. Is this what is was liked to be gassed by the apposing army during, world war? Yes, even worse inside and out, and Dad was driving. I could stick my head out even further, this seemed to help some. We could not stop and freeze, we had to carry on, through the night.

At last daylight was breaking and we were arriving at Discovery Mine. In an upper bunkhouse they had beds for truckers. We could not eat, we were totally gassed.

We laid in bed, passed out immediately. I awoke, it was now dark again. I was out, close to 24 hours. I had the most severe head ache, I was sure my head had split in two. I looked across at Dad. Dad was not moving. I could not hear him breathing. I at 11 years old, knew nothing about how to take a pulse, still I tried, nothing. I pinched him and pulled at him. No response, this went on for 2 hours. I would give up and lie on my bed. Cry. And then start again. Try to get a response. I cryed, bawled like a 2-year-old baby. Then Dad stirred. Wow. Is he alive? I remember the caribou moving in the bombardier. I thought the caribou was alive and about to get up. Dad at that time, told me "It's only nerves, and it was only nerves, the caribou was dead. Is this, only nerves or is Dad alive? A few minutes later dad woke up, he too, with the most splitting headache of his life.

CHAPTER 17

BRUCE WEAVER, BILL FOLKS, JOHN H. PARKER, NORMAN W. BYRNE.

The winter I turned 14, in January, Bruce Weaver gave me a job, stocking the store shelves after school and Saturdays. With School out in June, I asked Bruce Weaver for a 2 month leave of absence. I had been offered a job, by Mannix Construction, a Calgary firm. They were building the Mackenzie Highway into Yellowknife. Yellowknife was to have road access to the south of Canada. I was offered a job doing dishes at the construction camp, at Snare River, 50 miles distance from Yellowknife. They were offering me $50 per month.

It was there I learned the most important lesson of my now plus 50 years, working career. 14 years old I was hired to do dishes. There were 3 of us feeding 50 men. The cook, the assistant cook and myself. We 3 had beds in a small adjoining Trailer. One night the cook and the assistant got into the booze. Their friend had returned from Yellowknife with several bottles. They drank until 3:00 am. So very noisy, but eventually I fell asleep.

The cook woke me at 4:00.

Said "Len. Will you cook breakfast" He had showed me how to make pancakes. He said "Len, if you cook breakfast, I will do your dishes". I said "ok" I cooked. Then it was time for the job of the assistant cook, to serve breakfast. I went into the trailer to wake him up.

He said "Len, if I give you $5.00 will you serve the men." Making $50 per month, $5.00 was 10% of my monthly wages, he had offered, I had not asked, but it turned out, that was irrelevant.

When it was time to do dishes, I went back into the trailer to wake up the cook.

I said "ok, you can now do the dishes"

The cook said "no!" I washed the dishes.

To my surprise about 4 hours later, Bill Folks, the top man, the manger of this road construction came to me.

He said, "Len. You are fired!"

"Why?"

Bill "because they had to pay you extra."

"What?" "they kept me awake all night and then I cooked, served, prepared 50 men's lunches and washed the dishes. You hired me to do dishes"

I said "give me a second chance, I will do anything"

Bill "I never give a man, a second chance."

From that day on, I decided, I will do anything, I will work the hours I am assigned and then some extra.

Dad reinforced this. Dad said, "Len if there are 10 men there and only one shovel, be sure you have the shovel." This lesson I learned well, served me well, when I went to work for Norman w. Byrne, 2 years later and served me well, all my life.

I had the remainder of the summer, to do nothing, had a great time. My dad was Foreman/ Operator for a subcontractor on this job, hence we had a one room cabin at the camp. My brother and I spent our days playing on the nearby, Snare River. There was a native fishing camp, 2 cabins at the river. They had left some very small, one person, paddle canoes at the water. The canoes were made of about 2 yards X 2 yards of canvas stretched over some willow sticks. The willow sticks were first joined, shaped in the form of a canoe about 2 yards long, next the canvas was stretched over this. One wrong move and the canoe would tip over, but the summer water was warm. We got very good at paddling these little canoes.

CHAPTER 18

TEACHING THE TEACHERS

Teaching the teachers, My Wynne and Mr. Robson. September came and was time to return to Yellowknife and school. Two new teachers, to Yellowknife had come from England. I told Mr. Wynne of our escapades during the past summer, specifically all the fish we did catch, whenever we wanted, by setting nets across snare river.

This caught Mr. Wynne's attention. "How do you set a net?" "Where do you go?" "How does this work?" "Are you licensed?"

I answered "Snare River, 50 miles along the highway, Yes, we are trappers, hunters"

One day, Mr. Wynne said "Len, if I supply the car, can go to Snare River and set nets"

"Yes, what day do you want to go?" We decided on Wednesday after school, I asked Bruce Weaver, for permission not to come into the store on Wednesday after school.

I told my brother, Mike, "Wednesday we are going to teach Mr. Wynne and Mr. Robson how to fish."

Wednesday, after school, the 4 of us climbed into Mr. Wynne's car and by 4:30 we were at Snare River. Mike and I put the net into these canoes.

Mr. Wynne "You can not get in those little canoes"

"Yes, we can, we have been paddling these little, floating canvas, all summer long"

Mike and I stretched the net across the river, as the two teachers watched. The fall run must have been on, the fish swimming up river. We left the nets set for about 2 hours and then started to remove the fish, the fish were swimming in as fast as we were taking them out. In these 2 hours we caught about 50 fish.

We split them 4 ways each taking an equal amount. We had taught our teachers how to fish. I told Mr. Wynne, the Yellowknife River rapids is almost as good, One's net fills up relatively quickly.

We taught them well, to well. About 2 weeks later, Mr. Wynne told me, told me they had made a second trip to Snare River.

I said "You, can not go without me, I have the license." (My Parents being trappers, we children inherited the same rights.)

Mr. Wynne said "Yes, we can, a law left over from the days school teachers in small communities had to obtain their own food."

On this Mike and I were out of luck, Mr. Wynne with the car, could go fishing whenever he liked. Mike and I were not yet, old enough to drive a car.

This year was the end of grade 9, in June school was out. During that summer, I saw Mr. Wynne, Mr. Robson one more time. Off in the distance, as we were in our skiff, heading for the Yellowknife

River rapids, off in the distance, in a skiff of their own they were returning from the rapids. I taught them well.

"The teacher hasn't taught until the student has learned." Perhaps I was a better teacher, than they. They were using both of my fish holes. That September I stated at the other school, High School, Sir John Franklin.

CHAPTER 19

LEARNING TO OPERATE HEAVY CONSTRUCTION EQUIPMENT

I would also go hunting with my dad. During the summer of these years, Dad had his job being part of the crew, operating equipment, building the Mackenzie highway to connect Yellowknife with the Canada's south.

During the winter Dad was hired to run motor grader, to keep this same road open, Tractor Trailers, Freightliners were now using this road to supply the town of Yellowknife. On Sundays I could go with Dad, learn how to operate the Motor Grader and we carried a rifle, in case we saw a wood caribou or a moose. This day, we did see a moose. Dad was operating, I was sitting to the right of him. I had not yet loaded shells into the rifle. I was trying to load it quickly.

Thank God! I had it pointed to the floor and not in the direction of dad or myself. BANG! I HAD JUST SHOT A 30, 30 RIFLE THOUGH THE FLOOR. So very many people have been killed in the North, with gun accidents.

Dad did not get excited. The grader, motor was loud and the grader blade scaping the road made plenty of noise, but, louder than a church bell, the rifle shot rang through the grader Operator's, our cabin. Our ear's still ringing.

Dad "did you just shoot a hole through the floor?" I guess dad thought, there was no need to "reem my butt", I had just learned my lesson, and we were both still alive. Needless to say, the moose was long gone, by this time.

Empty guns kill! Mom had told me, never point a gun at yourself or anyone. She told me of a story, she had returned from hunting, believed she had emptied her gun before entering the house, playing, pointed the gun at her brother, then questioned herself. "Did she empty, the gun?" Pointed the gun to the floor, pulled the trigger and fired a bullet into the floor. Was this sub-concisely in my mind that day in the Motor Grader. Thank god, I had the gun pointed to the floor.

Those years after the road, Mackenzie Highway, was built to the outside world I did get to travel that highway. I guess, I must have been 15 years of age when, Smokey Heal decided, I should know Edmonton, Calgary. To represent Yellowknife, Smokey, was putting together a team of 8 Riders, to ride in the Parade. The Parade at the Calgary Stamped. Smoky asked me if I ever rode a horse.

I said "yes, when I was nine years old." My grandfather owned, probably the only 4 horses, north of the 60th parallel.

CHAPTER 20

YELLOWKNIFE'S "BEVERLY HILLBILLIES"

Smokey said "Ok, come to Edmonton / Calgary with us." This is how I came to ride, in the Calgary Stampede Parade.

The second day of driving, we arrived in Edmonton, near 10pm. Driving down Jasper Avenue, 10:00 in the evening, early July. it started getting dark. I remember how it stuck me! Like a light, going "pop" in my head. WOW, It really does get dark in the evening! In the South, there really is no 24-hour sun/ daylight. The other things that struck me, I had, of course, never saw a train before, as the train passed us, it went on and on, so very big and long. I had never saw a herd of cows before, there were so many. There must be many more cows than the buffalo, occupying the land, when Christopher, arrived here.

We spent a day or two in Edmonton, then a day, at Smokey's brother farm, this was most interesting, pigs, chickens, all things I had never saw before, then onto Calgary.

I do not know how, but seems Smokey, knew most everyone in Calgary. The following day I was assigned my horse, the one I would ride in the Parade. We, all 8 Riders, were all dressed in black pants, yellow shirts, Yellowknife colors, with big, Yellowknife signs. People cheering, a great introduction for a young man, from the North, to the outside world.

Telling my Parents, the events of this trip, motivated my Dad, to do the same thing the following year. I have to tell you this was a different, but still an interesting experience. There is a Country and Western song, "Always be Humble and Kind" Yes, One learns these traits. Humility.

It was about this time that Yellowknife, got it first television, but it was canned programs. Old Television programs, show in a building uptown.

The Beverly Hillbillies: Dad could not afford hotel rooms. Dad made a camping trailer. Dad got an old axle from a wrecked vehicle. Dad welded a frame on this axle and built a platform out of boards. This became the floor of our camper. Next Dad built a plywood box about one foot high, the walls of our camper. On this he pitched a tent. Down in the day, up at night. Each night, Dad would pitch a separate tent for us older kids. We did not stay in regulated camp grounds. Dad would pick a vacant field on the side of the road and here is where we would pitch our tents, for the night.

Pulling this home-made plywood trailer, behind our car, camping in fields, I am certain, we were entertainment, laughing stock, for anyone seeing us, but have to admit, we had a good time. Once again, went to the Calgary Stamped. Our Vancouver Island cousins joined us in Calgary. Dad had not seen his brother, since he was nine. At nine, Dad's parents separated. My grandfather took dad to the Arctic. Raised by my grandmother, they had moved to Vancouver Island. My Uncle Mike, got an education, seemed very sophisticated. We all, the two families drove to Vancouver Island, where Dad saw the mother, he had not seen since he was nine. My Cousins had a real house, with running water, an indoor bathroom and all the modern conveniences. Possibly made my mother a little envious. Dad's response was "yes, he does not go outdoors to the toilet at 40 degrees below zero, well he probably has a big mortgage."

Today, each time, I sit on my bidet, and shoot warm water, onto my butt, somehow memory of sitting on a carved out of a plank at 40 degrees below zero, pops back into my mind. The comparison. I like this much better.

On our way home to Yellowknife. One night in Alberta, we were camped in a Farmers field. I had never seen a lightening, thunder, and then rain, like this, Bang, Bang and louder thunder, the flash from Lightening, our whole tent was light up like daylight all night long. I expected the next lighting strike would definitely hit our tent. Flat field, and lighting striking the ground all around us. We were the highest point on the landscape. How it never hit us? God was looking after us!

Like so many times in my life, for so many reasons since, I did not know whether to be scared or thrilled.

My whole life since, always feeling I was out of my league, yet always looking for the next challenge!

There were more trips to the outside world, Edmonton, with Smokey Heal. Smoky Heal, was one of those wonderful people, every town has, Smokey was involved in organizing everything. One of the things he was involved in was organizing Sled Dog team Races, in Edmonton. With my Uncles winning most of the Canadian Championship Dog Derby's, Mike and I would also get invited along, each "Dog Musher" had a helper at the starting line and Mike and I certainly knew "Dog Mushing" Our Uncles and others wanted our help. We would get to miss a week of school. The most memorable trip, we were invited to the home of one of the Edmonton

Dog Mushers. We did not have Television in Yellowknife. For most of the world, the Beatles on the Ed Sullivan show was something to see. For Mike and I it was doubly memorable, our first exposure to television and this was the night, the Beatles were appearing on Ed Sullivan. I remember it like it was yesterday.

The following day, 16 years of age, I was to take part in the Men's 20-mile snowshoe race. There were racers from everywhere, the army, also from numerous towns, in Alberta and Saskatchewan. I placed fourth. I thought 4th. was bad. Uncle Danny came to me "Len, I am so proud of you, you placed 4th and you are not even sweating" It made the Yellowknife Newspaper, my teachers read it. I would be anyway, but now I had to be especially important to be honest about why I missed a week of school.

I have since travelled the world. I have often held jobs, far beyond what I ever expected, dreamed. More interesting, than what initially appeared to be my life, my destiny.

CHAPTER 21

SMASHING INTO THE RCMP AIRPLANE

"Driving truck in Yellowknife, playing hockey for the Yellowknife Indians hockey team."

I turned 16. Thanks to my friend Danny Pappas and his father George Pappas, I had the job with Precambrian Mining Services, a subsidiary of Norman w. Byrne Limited. I had my driver's licence, my job was to drive around town, the different stores in town, pick up the food supplies, the exploration requirements and the mining supplies and load these items on the bush airplanes. I loved this job. I guess I did it well, because, fall came, time to return to school. John parker, Shorty Brown, asked me if I wanted to stay on, work for them after school and Saturdays. I said Yes, Yes, Yes! I worked for them for 6 years, every holiday, after school and Saturdays, until I graduated from Haileybury School of Mines. Mostly everything was "rosy."

What was not so "rosy" was I also worked for Byers Transport every opportunity I got. Fall and Spring of the year I could work after dinner for Byers Transport. I would go to school, leave school at 3:30. Work at Precambrian Mining until 6:00. Eat for ½ hour, 6:30 to midnight work for Byers Transport. This would have been the second year, I being 17.

The Mackenzie Highway to Yellowknife had now been completed a couple years. Most material was being trucked into Yellowknife from Edmonton in the south. The problem was the crossing of the Mackenzie River at Fort Providence. In the summer months a ferry was used. Trucks drove onto the boat and crossed the river. In the winter there would be an ice road across the river, however what to do between that time there were to much ice on the river for the boat to cross, yet the ice was not yet, strong enough to carry loaded transport trucks?

In the town of Hay River, airplanes were loaded with the food supplies, those perishable and urgent supplies, loaded in Hay River and unloaded in Yellowknife. After dinner 6:30 Byers would put a crew together to unload these planes, deliver this freight.

One night, disaster struck. Every Fall, there would be a RCMP, Policeman's ball in Yellowknife. Many of the RCMP were pilots. They would from all the northern communities fly their Twin Otter Dehavaland aircraft to attend the ball. They had a twin otter sitting on the edge of the airstrip close to the area, we, the other Byers employees and myself, were unloading Wardair's Bristal airplane.

The first truck was now full, I got into the driver's seat to move it to the edge of the strip, out of the way so we could back in the second truck to be loaded. Pitch black night. This night seemed to be especially black, no moon, no northern lights, dancing in the sky. A Pitch, Black night! Perhaps I was to tired. Bang!, I was stopped, but what? Why? I still did not realize I had hit the wing of the RCMP, airplane. In the fall of the year, the snow is on the airstrip but not yet, deep. I though I had just hit some deeper snow, where the plow trucks would have piled it on the edge on the tarmac, while plowing the airstrip. I backed up. Thinking I had to get a longer run at it to get through the snow ridge, I gunned it, petal to the metal. Charged again. Again bang! I was stopped. I HAD HIT THE

RCMP AIRPLANE, BACKED UP AND TOOK ANOTHER RUN AT IT! Who would believe it was an accident? I assure you it was, but even today, when I think about it, I can hardly believe it myself. The Inspectors drive up and look at that mess, they would swear, I had something against the RCMP.

John Parker, my boss at Precambrian Mining was also the Yellowknife Mayor. He was at the policeman's ball, that night.

The local business men were also invited, Byers night supervisor at the plane unloading, had to call Byers management, Johnny Dennison, who was at that hour attending the Policeman's ball. No cell phones in those days, yet, within 15 minutes, everyone in town knew an RCMP airplane had been hit.

Needless to say, Byers never called me to help again, but I was also worried about my Precambrian Mining, after school job. I stressed about it all day in school. Do I still have my job at Precambrian Mining. I need that job. I need the money now and I need to save for University. After school, as usual, I went to work, went to Precambrian Mining. I did not say anything, I simply started to work. After a short time, John Parker walked by. Was he making conversation or was he testing me? He knew my Dad worked for Byers transport. Did he know, I also worked for Byers, after dinner?

Everyone in town was talking about it, seemed the only thing anyone talked about for the next few days.

John said "Len did you hear Byers Transport ran into the RCMP airplane last night?"

I hesitated thinking, I have to, come clean, I hope John does not fire me.

I said "I was driving the truck, I went on to explain to John how it happened."

To my surprise and relief, John said "Len, you must stop working so hard"

I said "well, I guess I have no choice about that, I expect, they (Byers) are not going to call me back"

The first summer working for Precambrian Mining, they kept me in town loading bush planes, for the exploration camps and mines, the next 5 summers, they sent me into the bush, to the exploration camps each summer, Christmas and Easter Holidays.

CHAPTER 22

MINING CLAIM, STAKING RUSH.

The year I was 17, I was sent to a camp on the south shore of Great Slave Lake, there were 4 of us in this camp. John Larkin, Donny Byrne, son of the owner Norman w. Byrne, a German University Student and myself. I being the youngest. Our job was to, with axes, cut lines, paths, a grid through the forest, so the following year, an Induced Polarization (I.P. Survey) study could be carried out. We divided into two groups, John Larkin and myself forming one group. We would race the other two, to see who could cut the most, who could clear the greatest distance of forest growth, to create these required paths. John and I normally won. We would run through the forest, our axes swinging. Long summer days, we could cut "a lot of line". About once per week the bush planes would bring us fresh grocery supplies.

On this day, my axe Partner, John had to return to camp early, to meet the airplane. I carried on alone, blazing trail, coming to the end of the day. I decided, I made the error of taking a short cut home, back to camp. This cutting line was very exhausting work. The summer sun was hot, very hot, beating down on us, we had to dress with jackets, hats to fend off the mosquitos, that came out of the muskeg, with each step came at us like a swarm of killer bees.

Each step woke another swarm. I was very tired, I would take the short cut back to camp. I knew that if I hit the lake shore to the east of camp, I could follow the lake shore back into camp. I set out walking. Walked and walked, long summer days, still it was now getting dark, how long had I walked? Why had I not come to the lake? What could I do, to spend the night out here, the mosquitos would eat me alive. There were bears, every now and again, we could encounter a bear, the bear and we would each go in separate directions, but if they came upon me when I was sleeping, what would they do?

The fact that I am writing this. Yes, I am still alive, few of the young men, I grew up with, are still alive. Many who grow up in Yellowknife become miners or bush pilots. Both these take as many young men, as a war zone.

Then I found what I hoped was the answer. I came to a swamp, with one high single tree in the middle. If I could climb that tree, I could possibly see the lake. I made my way through the swamp to the tree, climbed the tree. I could see the lake. The Lake was behind and off to the left of me. I had walked to far inland, right past the camp. I arrived back at the camp as the night was getting black. That fall told dad, about how I got lost, in the woods.

Dad said "Anybody who says they never got lost in the woods, has not spent much time in the woods."

Those were the days before map staking. In those days, people still had to walk through the bush and blaze a mark of trees, to obtain the mineral claims.

Fall of the year, I had turned 19, I went off to Edmonton to Alberta College. Middle of December, I got a phone from John Parker, Precambrian Mining.

"Len are you coming home for Christmas?"

"No John, I can not afford the airfare."

John answered, "We want to stake a confidential area on Indian Lake, if you will come home, spend your holidays, staking claims for us, we will pay you $25 per day, plus pay your airfare." "They offered me 3 X what they normally paid me. $25 per day, that is over, $3.00 per hour, great wages for those days. (Years, later this became a mine.)

"Yes, I will come home for Christmas."

I was on Indian Lake, through Christmas, through New Years, myself and my helper, Freddy Diamond C. 44 below zero, New Years eve, my sleeping bag, sleeping in my 3 star eiderdown in a tent.

Everyone made their bed from a pile of spruce branches. In this extreme cold, we did not sleep on cots, sleeping on cots the air would circulate 360 degrees around us. The cold would go through your whole body. Also, we did not sleep directly on the frozen ground. We would cut many Spruce Brough branches. The spruce needles are soft. The wood, branches hard. The idea, the most comfortable sleep, was weaving the bigger end, the sticks, under the smaller ends, the needles. This made a comfortable base on the frozen ground. The pile of branches between the frozen ground and my sleeping bag.

Laying in my sleeping bag, I reached up wrote on the tent, ceiling, "New Years Eve 1965, 44 degrees below Zero. Indian Lake."

Christmas holidays were soon over and I returned to Edmonton to complete the first semester. The first semester completed at the end of January.

Then came another phone call, near middle of January, John was on the line. John Parker, Precambrian Mining is on the line for you. I took the call.

"Len, come home at the end of this semester. There is a staking rush going on and we need you here." Pine Point Mine had been discovered, but now a junior company, Pyramid Mining has made a huge discovery on the adjoining property. Everyone, who knows how to stake a claim is heading for the town of Hay River, the hotels are full, people are pitching tents everywhere. I wrote my first semester exams and got on a Plane. We staked claims through the month of February.

After the claims were staked, they needed to be drilled. Boyles Brothers were the North's main diamond drilling company. Are their more alcoholics in the north, or did it just seem that way, when One looked at the community that made up the Diamond Drillers. Bottom line: Most of the diamond drillers were alcoholics. These fellows would go into the bush, drill for a few months and return to Yellowknife. The full time they were in Yellowknife, they would be drunk, and soon broke. Although, I was by far the youngest person on the job, the company made me Party Chief, not because, I knew the job, but because they knew I would be sober. After arriving in camp, the drillers would have "the shakes" for a few days. During these days I would get the camp, tents set up and get the job organized.

The fact I was Party Chief on Diamond drill jobs, was to, very much help me later in life. These words shaped my whole life. To my surprise, this, these words, on my resume is what caught the attention of the Iron Ore Company of Canada, recruiter. Many Recruiters, from many mining companies, came to Hailey bury School of Mines, that spring. I was a second year, graduate, when offered the best job, any recruiter, had to offer. Second year graduates were Mining Technicians. Third year graduates were Mining Technologists. I was hired over many third year graduates, whom applied for this job.

With the drilling job under way, I was then moved to the Deep Arctic which was still well frozen. John Larkin and I were sent to the area, of what later became the Lupin Mine. Is this where I came closest to losing my life? John and I set up our tent on the lake, near the lake shore. These tents 10' x12', by 8 feet high at the peak, a person could put a wood stove in the corner. John started setting up the tent.

I said, "John are we setting up the tent right on the lake ice."

"Yes, we will have a flat floor" "We will put a lot of spruce boughs on the floor, heat rises, so we will not melt the ice." "That little that does melt while we are cooking dinner will freeze while we are sleeping and after breakfast freeze again, while we are staking claims during the day.

John was right, the lake ice never melted under our wood stove, but getting wood almost cost me my life.

We were in the far north. The only wood available to feed our stove, was in a ravine about 3 miles from our tent. When the wind starts to blow, the snow in the arctic, like a sand storm in the Sahara, you can not see. It is a complete "white out"

The storm was now into it's third day. We were out of, we had burned the last stick of wood. I thought, I have been to the wood ravine often enough, I can feel my route by the terrain, the lay of the land.

"I will simply leave from behind our tent and go straight"

I got on the ski-doo, pulling the sleigh behind, intending to load the sleigh with wood. After about 1 mile, I realized this was not working. I was lost. Once again, I was lost, very lost. I turned the ski-doo around and tried to follow my tracks back. Sitting on the ski-doo I could not see the tracks. I got off and started walking looking down at the ground but the wind, whirling, howling, blinding, blowing snow had completely erased my tracks. I dug a hole in the snow, in effect made an igloo about the size of my body. I was soon becoming very hungry, back at the tent I had my warm bedroll and food. What was I doing here?

If I am anywhere near where I think I am, if I walk off to the left, I will come to the shore of the lake. I can then follow the Lake shore back to the tent. I started walking, because of snow drifts the surface of the lake was not that flat. All of a sudden, I realized, said under my breath "I am walking on the lake. How long have I been walking on the lake?"

I turned around found I had only walked a short distance on the lake. If this is the right lake, I can return to the tent. It was the right lake.

The craziest of all, should have known better. All I saw was dollar signs. A wolverine is the most valuable pelt in the north. The pelt of a wolverine does not frost up. Put around the hood of a parka, wolverine fur will not frost up, from a person's breath.

By now the camp had grown, there were 10 of us in camp. We were 5 crews divided into work teams of 2 men. My Partner was a fellow, probably 10 years older than I, he was behind me. on the back of my ski-doo. He was from the village of Snowdrift, never went to school, hunted all his life. In the Barren lands, there are some ravines, different areas where stunted trees grow at random, about 10 or20 feet apart. Trees about 8 to 10 feet tall were now in about

6 feet of snow. The morning, we were heading in the direction of our work area.

I saw this wolverine, wow, how many dollars is that pelt worth. With the Ski-doo, I started to chase the wolverine. My Partner, on the back was yelling STOP! Stop! Are you crazy.

He kept yelling.

I kept chasing. I wanted that pelt. He mostly skipped, on top of the 6 feet of snow, I was sinking about a foot but, no problem. I caught up to the wolverine. The wolverine dodged. I went over it tail and possibly a little of it's back, but as it only sunk into the deep snow, it really did not notice. It was now, charging away, off to my left. Did not realize it at that moment, but it could have turned around and grabbed, chomped down, my leg, with their strength, broke it in two. The wolverine was running and I was chasing. But now I was some distance from him, it took me longer to turn and go in his direction. He could turn immediately. Turning the ski-doo in this deep snow took a little longer. My Partner was more than ever, yelling! Stop the chase, stop! Stop! I ignored him, I wanted this pelt.

I was now again, going in the same direction of the wolverine and gaining on him once again. I hit a tree. The top of one of these trees that stick out of the snow. I was stopped. The wolverine was gone. Now I was listened to my Partner.

"If you had caught him. If you had run over him, in this deep snow, he would only sink, you would not have hurt him. He would have killed both of us."

"Shit! What was I thinking? You are so right!"

September came Norman w. Byrne stopped me in the office. The Norman W. Byrne Company, occupied the front of the building. Precambrian Mining occupied the back of the building. Both companies were owned by Norman w. Byrne.

"Len, what are you going to do this fall?"

"Nothing, play hockey for the Yellowknife Indians and continue working for you, this is what dad wants me to do." There were only 6 teams in the National hockey league." With so many NHL teams today, Players, who would today make the National Hockey League, were available to work in the Mines. All the Mines wanted the best hockey team. Ontario Mines, Quebec mines, and Yellowknife, Giant mine, and Con mine. Anybody who could play hockey, were offered jobs, of some sort, in the mines. Hence there were 3 very good hockey teams in Yellowknife. Con Cougars, Giant Grizzles and Yellowknife Indians.

Norm, Mr. Byrne, to me, said "No, Len, you are going to Haileybury School of Mines"

"No, I can not, I have not saved enough money"

Mr. Byrne asked, and I told him how much I had saved.

"Len, the North West Territorial Government, recently introduced a program to help children of the north, get a college, university education, down south." With what you have saved and this stipend, you can do it"

Mr. Byrne got on the phone, called the Dean of Haileybury School of Mines. "I have one more student for you.

The Dean "send him down."

Next Mr. Byrne called the Territorial Government and arranged my monthly stipend. I was a couple days later, on an airplane south. Learned a lot, and made a lot of friends, still friends today, that first winter.

I was so very shy, in those days, the way I grew up, gave me confidence, at the same time, possibly? No, not possibly, definitely! made me feel a little inferior. Mike had bought a car. We drove to the "outside world" In Edmonton we had to stop at a government office, get our first check, our monthly North west Territories stipend, for attending college in the south. My class mate, Brian McCleod, drove south with us, picking up his check. I did not hear myself speaking. I asked for my check. I remember this so clearly. Brian said "Len, why do you always talk in a whisper, when talking to adults." I overcame it. I do not talk in a whisper today.

In the spring I was back working for Precambrian Mining. That was the last time, I worked, lived in the North West Territories. I did years later do a fly in, fly out, to the Diamond Mines, from my home in Vancouver.

There are 3 professions, the World can not do without. Of Course, Teachers, Farmers and Miners, Without Farmers we do not eat. Without Miners, Farmers do not have the tools, they need to farm and Teachers to teach these and all other professions. I have mined, Iron Ore, Asbestos, Uranium, Coal, Tar Sands, Gold, Diamonds, Copper, anything that is economical.

This spring, it was Uranium, the investors would pay for exploration programs for uranium.

Finished Haileybury, for the year on May 14, and a couple days later I was back in the bush north of Yellowknife. Uranium was the flavor of the World's economic cycle, that spring. Investors pick different metals, for which they want to finance at different times in the cycles. Brice Mercredie and I were sent with north east with Geiger Counters, hand carry uranium detection units. Each day we would walk a grid during the day and walk across the lake to out tent camp at the end of the day. To walk around the lake would take, twice as long. Each day we could see the ice candling. Everyday we would walk to the edge of the lake, and make, a decision, the warm days were melting the lake ice. This day Brice said, he had enough, he was taking no more chances, he was walking around the edge of the lake. I felt it was still ok, I would try the shortcut across, one more day.

It was a foolhardy decision. About 2/3 of the way across the lake, I came upon very candled ice. Before I realized it, I was going down. Down through the ice, water was now up to my waist. I threw my upper body forward, on my stomach, flat on the ice. It was holding me. My body, much bigger than the soles of my feet reduced the pounds per square inch, on the ice surface. I am going to be ok? I slid on my stomach, my body forward, I was making progress, I was getting out of the hole, I had created. Going across the ice on my stomach, I came to ice not as badly candled. I was able to get up and walk the rest of the way back to our tent. That was close enough. The next day, I walked with Brice. I stayed on land, walked around the shore.

CHAPTER 23

OPEN PIT MINING

After graduation, Haileybury School of Mines, I was offered a job at Iron ore Company of Canada. (IOC) Schefferville Quebec. My resume caught their attention. The were particularly impressed with the fact, I had been Party Chief on Diamond Drill jobs. Schefferville in Northern Quebec, is above the tree line, in the Barren Lands of Canada. Seemed each time the company had an opportunity to hire someone from Yellowknife, they did so. Before me, Bill Knutson, Jed Dagenias, Gee Dagenias, Don Byrne, (son of Norman W. Byrne) and others. IOC Offered me a Forman Trainee's job. The offered a year's training, but after about 2 weeks in Schefferville, the bosses, gave me my own crew of about 40 men.

"Len, you already know most of the things we were going to teach you." The years I had spent sitting at my dad's side learning how to operate Heavy construction machinery was paying off.

The Schefferville Mine may have been one of the largest mines in the World, at the time. The numerous Iron ore, open pits stretched out for over 50 miles. Trains of 100 ore cars entered the numerous pits.

In the following years the copper, coal, tar sands, Open Pit mines, of western Canada, were to open, up. Experienced in large Open Pit

Mines, the fellows who had been my mentors at Iron Ore Company of Canada, were offered the management jobs in western Canada. From my mentors I started to get phone calls.

"Len, we are constructing, opening this mine, come and work with us." As a result, I may have started, been involved in more mine start up than, possibly anyone.

My two older children were born in Schefferville. While working at Schefferville, I received a job offer, from Anaconda Copper Mining Company, Anaconda owned much of the country of Peru. I initially accepted the job. I wanted the opportunity of foreign experience. The company wanted medical exams on all 3 of us. My older child, recently born, my wife and myself. We went to the Schefferville hospital, doctor's office. I had my medical. Diane had her medical. Now it was our new born son's turn. The doctor had to take Derrick's blood. He was coming at Derrick, with what seemed to my wife, a needle as big as Derrick.

My wife turned to me, said "you big Meany!"

I said "Stop!" "Stop!" The doctor stopped.

I phoned Anaconda and said "I will not be coming to, Peru" Years later I did end up going to Peru, I have now been working in and out of Peru 23 years.

I worked at Iron ore Company of Canada, one more year, when I received a phone call from Jim Murdock, General Manager, at Cassiar Asbestos, asking me if I wanted the job of General Foreman/ Mine Captain. The Clinton Mine, Northern Yukon, north of Dawson City, short distance from the arctic circle.

Great, Responsible for the mine 24 hours per day, I will no longer have to work, shift work. No more night shifts for me. This will be an easy interview. Jim Murdock and Terry Ferderber, were going to be interviewing me. Jim Murdock, like me, got his start at Iron Ore Company of Canada, years earlier and Terry Ferderber, Mine Superintendent was Haileybury School of Mines alumni An easy interview, I got the job. I was still 24, would turn 25 in two weeks. I had Foremen and Operators with up to 30 years experience, working for me. There were a number, of people, who were unhappy about this.

None as unhappy as Don Hodgeon, the Assistant Mine Superintendent, who was to be my immediate boss. For some reason, he was not invited to interview me. The company moved my family across Canada, from Northern Quebec to Northern Yukon. I got a surprise, when, I arrived on the job. My boss was to be someone who did not have an opportunity to interview me. The lesson in this: Never accept a job, unless the person who is to be One's immediate boss, has the opportunity, to interview One. Four years I worked for Don. He hated me, most every day, I was aware of it. During those 4 years, he did give me one compliment. Don had been on holidays and extended by an upgrade course, he was to take at Queens University. Don was away for some time. When Don returned he looked around the mine, did a complete inspection.

Said "Len, you kept the mine running, your costs are good, you mined in the exact same sequence I would have."

I should have but did not return the compliment. Don was a very intelligent man. It may have been difficult, but I had learned a great deal, from him.

People get killed in Mines.

Strange the things you think of, when you really expect you are about to "meet your waterloo." The closest I came to meeting my waterloo on this Project, happened one day in March.

When One wakes up in the middle of the night, feeling stress, emotion, wondering "what is life all about, why is the night so dark" One say to themselves "well, what it's about, is not really important, just enjoy it" and One goes back to sleep.

When large mine haulage trucks drive up a ramp, the nose, the hood, of the truck, way out in front of the driver is also sloped upwards at 15%. A driver's vision is restricted, can not see, over the hood of the truck, those objects nearest in front of him. The driver can see off in the distance. The closest I came to "meeting my Waterloo" on this project was, I earlier in the day traded the mine maintenance foreman pickups. We were now about to trade back. Brian, the maintenance foreman, had parked my truck at the top of the ramp, directly in front of any loaded haulage truck, that came up the ramp. The Front End Loader had now loaded the truck and he was, grinding his way, coming up the ramp. Not thinking about the fact his hood was blocking his vision, I jumped into my pickup to move it off the haulage trucks path. It took a minute to start my pickup and the haulage truck kept coming. The big haulage truck tires, were now, pushing in my driver's door. The undercarriage, oil pan, of the haulage truck was squashing down the pickups roof. The far door would not open.

Derrick our older son, was now 2years old, Stacey-Lynn was 1year old. Our two children were 11 months apart.

The big haulage truck tires, were now, pushing in my driver's door. The undercarriage, oil pan, of the haulage truck was squashing down the pickups roof. The far door would not open. I knew I was dead, seconds more.

I was not afraid. Flashed through my head: I was thinking, well I have to go sometime, how is Diane going to pay for Derrick, Stacey-Lynn's university.

Then the haulage truck stopped moving. O god, I was saved. We all gathered around.

I asked the haulage truck driver "what made you stop?"

I had parked the second pickup, the one I had been driving earlier, Brian's pickup, on the level, about 40 feet beyond the top of the ramp, Brian, had gone, planning to get in this pickup, when he saw me being squashed. Apparently, Brian froze, as he saw me being squashed. The haulage truck driver could see Brian's eyes.

He said "I saw Brian's eyes, they were as big as saucers, I knew there was something wrong."

My Pickup was totaled but, I was ok. I would be able to pay for my children's university. "When I thought about it later, when I think about it today, what a strange thing to be thinking about"

When One wakes up in the middle of the night, there is possibly one emotion, when actually faced, with a situation, faced with reality, a different, things are totally different. Being happy, is making a decision, deciding to be happy.

In the Clinton Mine, we mined the ore and some portion of the waste with our company equipment. We contracted to General Enterprise Ltd. a portion of the argillite waste rock, stripping. General Enterprise used bottom load Scrapers for this job. The Scrapers would travel over the blasted Argillite, open their bottom and scrap up a load. The mine was near top of this mountain. The waste was dumped over the edge of the mountain. The scrapers would come to the waste dump, dump their load and return for another load. A Caterpillar dozer would push the load over the edge. The closer the scrapers could come to the edge the less work there would be for the Dozers. The Dozer operators were always complimenting the Scraper Operators who could dump closest to the edge. This one, night shift, one scraper operator came to close to the edge. His Scraper was still on top but partially hanging over the edge of the waste dump. The Operator was able to get off the Scraper. They contacted the night, shift foreman.

The night shift foreman looked at the Scraper, called a Dozer over and hooked a cable from the front of the Scraper to the back of the Dozer.

"Ok, he said to the Operator, "get back on there and steer it out as the Tractor Dozer pulls."

"You're not getting me, back on there, not on that 631 Caterpillar Scraper, not the way it is hanging, ready to fall over the edge." said the Operator.

The Shift Foreman, jumped into the Operator's seat, took the Scraper controls and signaled the Dozer Tractor to start pulling. As they moved the Scraper, instead of coming back upon the dump surface, went the rest of the distance over the edge. The Scraper was hanging, dangling on the tow cable, over the edge, spinning like a dog on the end of a chain. A near, 50 ton machine crushing the shift foreman's body with each, roll. I got a phone call, 3.00 am in the morning. Come to the mine, bring the doctor, bring the ambulance. Crushed beyond recognition. My wife went to console the Shift Foreman's wife, to be with her. Please be sure she does not hurt herself, nor their children. We need an airplane to bring her home to her family in Duck Lake. Saskatchewan.

CHAPTER 24

MIKE IS LOST

Not a good year. It was about this time that I got a phone call from mom.

"Mike is lost!"

"What?"

"He was flying from Edmonton to Yellowknife during a snowstorm, never arrived in Yellowknife"

I was 26 at the time, Mike was 24, the year before Mike called me up, "Len, I have about ½ the money I need to buy a bush airplane, will you loan me the balance." As General Mine Foreman of this arctic mine, the pay was excellent. The company provided most everything, heated home, free electricity, company vehicle. Most of my paycheck could go into savings.

I sent Mike the money he needed to buy his airplane.

"Mom, what should I do? Should I return to join the search?"

Mom said "The searching airplanes were mostly full. People were volunteering to be "spotters". To be "spotters" Hazel had returned from University. Dad and Linda had gone to the search area. Many others from Yellowknife and the communities further south were volunteering their time"

"No, Len, carry on working. We will inform you of any progress."

The search went on and on, no sign of Mike. One day the Air Force Search Captain came to dad "We are nearing the end of our allotted hours, make a decision, do you want to tighten the grid and re-fly the areas we have flown or do you want to increase the area."

Dad chose to tighten the grid. That spring, when the snow melted of the wings of the airplane, Mike's airplane was spotted from a plane flying overhead. Mike was found east of the search area. Seems as Mike realized he was in trouble, flew east looking to land on the highway. Guessing, he did not see the road nor railroad in the storm. He had landed on a slew, well east of these two landmarks, damaging the plane, on landing. Indications are, written notes, he lived about 3 weeks, as he froze to death.

Until dad passed away, he cursed himself, saying he made the decision that cost Mike his life. Saying he should have opted to increase the search area.

To this day, mom says, if only Mike smoked, he would have had matches to keep himself warm. Of course, we have no way of knowing either of these. For a young man, who knew the north, why? Why? Yet, so many of those, I grew up with are now dead!?

Over the years with each new mine "start up" in Western Canada, I would get a phone call, sometimes from Haileybury School of

Mines, Alumni, sometimes from my Mentors from my Iron Ore Company of Canada, days.

Not much to do in a community in the arctic, thirty families, and 400 men living in bunkhouses, company doctor, 4 school teachers. The pay checks were great, and the housing was free. Working for my paycheck and my next promotion. My Job was steady shift, yet at times of equipment was down, needed repairs or other situation in the mine, I would work until 1:00 or so in the morning. Not surprising that my first marriage ended in divorce. Take a 21year old girl from her mother, bring her to the barren, frozen, isolated communities of first Schefferville, then more isolated Clinton Creek. Work these long hours, bucking for my next promotion. Anyway, this night, I arrived home at 1:30 am.

CHAPTER 25

STARTING NEW MINES

Diane said "you got a call from Bill Kratz." Bill was Haileybury, Alumni. "Bill is down in Saskatoon, said to call him, regardless of what time you get home from work"

"Regardless, of what time, I got home from work, sounds urgent?"

I said it again. "He said to call him, regardless of what time?"

"Yes, that is what he said"

Near 2:00 am, I called Bill Kratz. "Hi Bill, it's Len here."

A sleepy, groggy, voice answered "Len, what are you doing calling me at this time of the night?"

"My wife said, you said to call you, regardless of what time, I get home from work"

"Yes, but not 2:00 am in the middle of the night." "Anyway, I am awake now. We are building a new uranium mine called Rabbit Lake, for Gulf Minerals, a division of gulf Oil. Do you want to come down here as Chief Engineer?"

The mining industry, all commodities, but especially the mining industry cycles, feast or famine. That same week Mike Joyce called me from Australia. Mike had been General Foreman at Iron Ore company of Canada, while I was Foreman Trainee, then Foreman. Mike was one of my mentors at IOC.

Mike Joyce had taken a job as Mine Superintendent, with Cliff Robe River, at their Iron Mine in Australia. Mike had recently been promoted to Mine Manager, and now needed a Mine Superintendent.

"Len are you interested in working with me again, as Mine Superintendent, here in Australia."

"Great. This would interest me."

"Ok, I know you but, others in the company will want to interview also, You need to fly to head office in Chicago."

I drove to Whitehorse and flew to Vancouver. I was in the Vancouver airport, when I heard my name mentioned over the intercom. On asking why, I told to call the Chicago office. I called the Chicago office.

"Len, there is no need for you to come the remaining distance to Chicago, Mike confirmed he wants you as Mine Superintendent. Mike is not interested in interviewing anyone else." "The job is yours."

I returned home to Clinton Creek, discussed with me wife, "what should we do?" "Which job do you want me to accept?" "Or should we stay here?"

We decided to, we did accept, the Chief Engineers job in Saskatchewan.

When we are planning to drive for a short vacation on a long week, holiday weekend, we listen to the radio, television: X number of people will be on the roads this weekend, hence statistics indicate there will be Y number of deaths, yet we drive, go visit relatives in other communities. "We believe, well I am not going to be one of those statistics" It is the same with starting a mine. The First Mine Manager always gets fired! If there is an exception, I am not aware of it. Yet seems everyone is willing to accept the Mine Managers job, on new start ups.

I was never Mine Manager, during a Start-up. I was normally hired to train, during Start-Ups. I operate most equipment, Underground and Open Pit. I have my blasting tickets for numerous provinces. That is not to say I never got fired. There are two dangerous times, if One is concerned about getting Fired.

One being Mine Start-ups, as I mentioned.

The second being, if your immediate boss quits, takes a job in a different mine or is fired, on those occasions One does not get promoted to fill his vacancy. On those occasions, when One is not promoted to fill the vacancy, your new boss is brought in from a distant mine, start looking for a new job, because your new boss will have favorites he wants to bring with him. As I have my mentors from my Iron Ore Company of Canada days, others have their mentors. Seems we miners move as a team.

This, my first of many mine Start-Ups, Gulf Minerals, Rabbit Lake Mine, was a routine mine start up. At this time, I have stated, been involved in starting 10 mines. Do all the planning, test the material in pilot plants. Design the Plant for the material, there are always surprises, the mine start ups never go as planned, function exactly as designed. In this mine, the designers decided the material was soft, a grizzly would be enough, a crusher was not needed. We started the mine in October, all the soft material after blasting would freeze into huge blocks. Freeze together and freeze plugging the holes in the grizzly. These surprises normally cost someone their job. Here the Mill Superintendent was fired first. After a period of time, the Assistant Mine Manager was replaced. Next the Mine Superintendent, taken out of the field, was sent to work in head office. It is embarrassing, never a reward to be given a desk job, in Head Office, better than being fired, but not a reward.

The mine, like all mines, we got "the bugs out" and the mine started to make the investors, Gulf Oil, money.

About that time, I found that several of my friends, mentors, from my Iron Ore Company days were working in the coal mines of Grande Cache, Alberta. Near 50% of the management in the maintenance department, also the operations and engineering department were ex IOC. They offered me a job as Superintendent of number 8 mine. The company, McIntyre Mines were mining with their own equipment in number 9 mine, but number 8 mine was being contracted. The offer, I could not refuse, substantially more than, I was making at Gulf Minerals, plus bonuses, one bonus for bringing the job in, under cost, a second bonus for staying until the end of the contract. Bonuses that would double my salary. We moved to Grande Cache. I did collect both bonuses.

Timing was perfect, as the contract at McIntyre number 8 mine, was being completed, Syncrude was starting up.

Another mine to start, my second, Syncrude was to be my second mine start up. After a mine starts, the Press Release always comes out "Under Budget and ahead of schedule" This is normally after the budget and the schedule has been revised about 3 times, and the start up has costed a sequence of one or two mine managers, their jobs. There are always surprises on mine start ups. The second or third Mine Manager, becomes the hero.

Mine start ups are not easy! Syncrude started with draglines and bucketwheels, after a time, shovels and trucks: Syncrude's Mel Farris was the first senior manager, to be fired. Start-ups are difficult.

Jim Carter became the hero. Jim felt draglines and bucketwheels were not necessary. Jim calculated pounds per square inch, of large trucks, large tires, felt and convinced the company, conventual Shovel / truck operations could work. Jim had numerous other good ideas. In addition, understood the political climate, within and without the company. Jim did substantial work with the neighboring native communities. Work they did, very well, Jim moved up through the ranks to President. Jim won Order of Canada, Mining Hall of Fame, Petroleum Hall of Fame.

During the third year of Syncrude start-up, I got a phone call from Paul Morrow, one mentor of my Iron Ore Company days. Paul asked me to return to Grand Cache, McIntyre Mines (Smokey River Coal), this time as Superintendent for the Mine Owners. The first time I had been there for a contractor. I enjoyed working for Paul. After about a year, Paul told me, "Len I accepted a position with Denison Mines, in Elliott lake." I was sorry to see Paul go. This time I did get the promotion, I became Mine manager. I was then 34 years old, I say, I became the youngest Mine Manager, ever of a major mine, in Canada, but I am not certain this is so. I believe, Jim Carter was 32, when he became Mine Manager. He may be the youngest Mine Manger of a major mine in Canada.

McIntyre Coal Mine (Smokey River Coal) is a difficult mine, high waste to ore stripping ratio, hence this mine becomes the world's emergency supply. Economics 101, Law of Supply and Demand. When the world is booming, more coal is needed, coal prices go higher, Smokey River Coal Mine is started up. Coal prices go down, Smokey River Mine is closed. Up and down, up and down over the years. My timing was bad, I became Mine Manager, a short time before the coal fields of north east British Columbia, The Quintette Coal and Bull moose Mines were coming on, was coming on stream. The Japanese had contracts to take their coal from these mines. Smokey River Mine was shut down.

Fortunately, my training, teaching ability, I was always in demand for new mine start ups. I was called to take on the Training Co-ordinator's position at Quintette Coal. This was my third mine start-up and the third mine, at which I was to train, the middle management and operators coming aboard.

Quintette Coal was the toughest start up yet. Each Mine manager, only lasted, as short time, Derik Rantz, Denny Miraz, John Saindon, others managers, were coming, being fired and going so fast, then Quintette Coal declared bankruptcy. It was years later on the second start-up that the design problems were to some degree, solved.

My dream, since I was walking down the streets of Yellowknife, at about 7, or 8 years old to start my own mine. It was time for me to pursue this dream. I went to Vancouver hoping to learn, how the stock exchange works. How do an IPO, an RTO.

The year was 1984. I arrived in Vancouver, not knowing what I did not know. It took years for me to learn, nobody wants to teach you, how the Exchange works. Fathers and Grandfathers will teach the next generation. It is a club! No one wants to teach a stray person who shows up in Vancouver/ Toronto saying "I too, want to start a mining company." "I too, want to make a million, learn how the Stock Exchange works?"

I began knocking on the doors of friends and acquaintances, I though may be able /willing to help me. I thought, the first thing, I need is a good potential mining property, something that has a possibility of making a Mine. I knew of some, but my buddy, from Haileybury school of Mines, Dave Duval, had been writing for the newspaper "The Northern Miner" for a number of years.

My thinking was, he would know every property in the World. For some reason, Dave was not the help, I had hoped he would be. Not sure why? Perhaps he was thinking "Len, you have no idea, what you are doing. Starting companies, understanding the gyrations of the Stock Exchange is completely different than starting mines."

I continued to bang on doors, meet people. I will never forget one of my early conversations, because of my extensive mining experience, even if they did not help, did not teach me, people were kind to me. I was invited to share an office on the third floor of the Royal Bank Building at the corner of Granville and Hastings. There were about eight junior mining companies, each in their own small office, surrounding a secretary in the center of the open floor. I looked at the properties, these companies owned, I thought most of them were garbage, the properties had no chance of ever becoming a mine.

I said, to the fellow, who invited me to share his small office. "Why are you promoting this shit, I know where you can obtain properties that have, some possible opportunity, to make the Investors money, to advance to a Mine."

The answer "blew me away."

He answered "If I ever discovered, I had a real property, I would not know what to do with it." He was not interested in having me help him, find a real, a legitimate property.

They years went on. Several times I had to return, work for the major mining companies, while I was learning, picking up little bits of information here and there, to one day start my own company. Do "my own" RTO or IPO.

This was fun but I had to return to work, to earn some money. Homestake/ Chevron partners, was starting an Underground Mine, in Northern British Columbia. Having spent my life in Open Pit Mines, to this point in time, I knew essentially, nothing of Underground Mines, worked 2 weeks at Madsen Red Lake during one Christmas holiday, while attending Haileybury School of Mines.

Sometimes it who you know, not what you know, that gets you the job.

Make friends with everyone, and never burn bridges, sometimes easier said than done, but make One's best efforts.

Anyway, Jed Digeneans is a friend of mine, older than me, while we were growing up in Yellowknife, but he was now, a graduate of University of British Columbia and was working at Iron Ore Company of Canada, Quebec, before I arrived. We became friends, while working here, Schefferville, Quebec. Ray Smith, who was to be Homestake's Mine Manger, and Jed Digeneans, had become friends while attending UBC. Ray asked Jed about me. Jed gave me a glowing recommendation, Ray hired me as Mine Superintendent at $44,000 per year.

I was the first of 3 to be hired by the company. Myself and two miners. Within weeks on the job, I actually us 3, thought we were about to "leave this world." The top of the mountain leveled off to rolling hills. We were on the side of the mountain, "collaring the portal" building the entrance to what would be the Underground Drifts (Tunnels). A short distance away on the next rolling hills we spotted a grizzly bear digging for rodents. Having experiences with Black Bears, and they mostly seemed to be harmless, we were not intimidated, but to the contrary, we were foolish. We waved our arms to get its attention, get a better look at it, take some pictures, yes, stupid. The Grizzly charged. He was down off his rolling hill, through the depression and onto our rolling hill, so fast, 55 miles per hour, cleared the distance in seconds. Being below the platform, in the depression we lost sight of the grizzly, he would have lost sight of us for a second, then with one bound, he was up onto the platform, ground we had leveled, in front of the portal. The grizzly, could have reached out a paw and taken off our heads, but as he seen the three of us and the tractor, he changed directions, went over the top of the portal. What made him change directions, change his mind? Why were we 3 still alive? A second before we were certain, we were dead. Certain in the next moment would be dead. This was the Golden Bear.

As the mine started, I soon realized including bonus, the Miners were making plus $75,000 per year.

I soon realized 2 things, although I was learning underground mining fast, I had a lot to learn. I did not initially have enough knowledge to be Underground Mine Superintendent. The second thing was, I could pick up a jack-leg drill, work as a Miner and make substantially more money. If I am going to be in this isolated mining camp, I may as well make as much money as possible. This I did, I moved down the hierarchy, to a Miner. Turning on the jack-leg was easy, I quickly learned how to make it "dance", break the most rock. In a short time, I was the third highest "bonus miner" of the 36 Miners.

Then the mine, shut down. The mine was badly designed, one would think a company like Homestake would have the expertise to build the best possible mine. Many mines, shut down, the first attempt to start them. It is not until the second, sometimes the third start-up before the mines make money. Engineers sit back, take a look at the design flaws in the first attempt. Redesign the Mine and start again. The company, Wheaton River, took control of this Golden Bear Mine. The second start up made the Investors money. I had long since moved on by the time of the second mine start up.

It was clear the Homestake, Golden Bear Mine, had to close down. I was holidaying in Yellowknife, I had gone home to visit, my family, my cousins, my mother. BHP was putting on a presentation, about their Diamond property, that evening. I had been following the diamond progress for some time.

A few years earlier, my mother had called me: "Len, there is a fellow up here (North West Territories), staking up, all the round lakes. What is he doing?"

I said "I do not know, he must be crazy" Telling this story to Chuck Fipkie a few years later, Chuck answered "there were times, when I also thought, I was crazy."

This evening in Yellowknife, BHP was putting on a presentation to inform the citizens of Yellowknife, their dreams, their objectives, if the drilling proved to be what they hoped. I entered the presentation; Bruce Turner of BHP was talking to the group. At Bruce Turner's side was Clem Pelletier. I had known Clem for about 20 years. Clem asked me "do you want to join the BHP team, build this diamond mine?" I being, a man, who knew the north, knew mining, many of the government officials were my cousins and extended family, Clem, introduced me to Bruce. Bruce immediately offered me the job, managing the underground portion of Ekati Mine. This was now my second Underground Mine and my 5th. mine start-up. This time I knew underground mining. I accepted.

Over the years, in conversations with, back home, talking to mom and the others, I was able to keep up on "The News". Those nights mom would call me late at night, I knew, I was prepared for bad news, someone who was important to me had passed on. No one has success in a vacuum. Without Ted Horton, Bruce Weaver, John Larkin, Shorty Brown, John h. Parker, Norman w. Byrne, I would not have had the life, I have enjoyed, and still enjoy, everyday.

Mom, would call me, she called me when Bruce Weaver, was killed in a hunting accident. Mom called me when, Norman W. Byrne passed away. Mom called me when John Larkin, Jim Magrum, Norman Byrne jr. were killed in a plane crash. These men had taken me "under their wing". I owed them, so much.

The memories come flooding back, I was so very close to John Larkin, we spent many hours running through the bush, slashing, cutting trees, out of the way, cutting trail for geophysical surveys. John was maybe 10 years older than me, John was in Haileybury School of Mines, those years, I was still in High School, the summer months, John wanted me and no one else as his Partner. John was always the Party Chief, until I got my turn. If the job required 2 men, it was John and I. If the job needed 10 or more men, it was still me, whom John took, "under his wing"

The news of the airplane crash devastated me. Seems a foggy, overcast day. Everything on the ground, the lake ice, the clouds, everything looked the same, the pilot though he was still well above the frozen lake, hence hit the ice with a severe thud. All four were killed. John Larkin, Jim Magrum, Norman Byrne jr. and the Pilot. So many, how is it possible that I am still alive?

BHP, Ekati Mine, this was my 5th. Mine start-up. We were drifting underground on two of the kimberlite pipes. Fox and Panda, but still had not received, the actual permitting for the mine. The start-up was taking longer than anyone anticipated. The biggest hurdle seemed to be the water use permit, or at least, officially it was the water use permit. Reality was the number of groups of natives, "what's in it for me"? Born in the North, my mother born on the Reserve, Fort Resolution, still I did not know there were so very many different groups of natives. Natives a thousand miles away, seemed to have an influence. I did not know there were so many different groups of natives. Get one group of natives on side and believe that we now had that problem solved, only to find the group had split into 2 an3 groups. Example: Growing up believing the Dogrib tribe were the group around Yellowknife. Get the Dogrib tribe on side and then find out. Oh, today, there is also a tribe called the Yellowknife tribe, start all over again. Groups and new splinter groups, there seemed to be, no end. I wondered, would the groups split and split, until each individual. Become their own tribe?

Waiting for permits was getting expensive, even for a company like BHP. BHP essentially shut down the camp for a period of time, kept minimum employees at the mine, worked from Yellowknife and Vancouver until mine permitting did come through.

I got a phone call from my brother-in-law, sister Hazel's husband "Len there is a Calgary group who own 50% of a potential mine in Quebec." Come to Calgary and talk to them. It all worked out, I was soon off to Quebec to start what was to be my 6th. mine start-up. A small one. The Croiner Mine near Val Dor. Permitting in Quebec, one had to jump through the same hoops, but there is no resistance, within 6months we were permitted. This was in middle 1990's. Gold was over $400 per ounce when we started. We went into production. Our break even was $330 per ounce, nearing the end of the 1990s gold fell to a low of $252.80 per ounce. We had to shut down the mine and wait. With me, there were 5Directors, the other 4Directors being Calgary Oil Men, the decision was shut down the mine, sell the property, turn the company into an Oil company.

The price of gold was down, Bre-Ex,(explained in the movie "Gold") had recently happened, Investors were not looking for an opportunity to finance gold, or any mining companies. It was impossible time to continue with my childhood dream of building "my own Mining Company". I went to Peru.

NEW CHAPTER 25

PERU

Murry Lytle, had gone to Peru, to open an engineering office for H. A. Symons, which is today AMEC. I was made aware Newmont/ Buenaventura's Mine, Yanacocha, wanted an experienced Open Pit mining man, to get costs down, production up. A short time later, I was working in Peru's Yanacocha Mine. Changing a few things, it was easy to get costs down, get production up.

I am proud to say, Canadian Mines Handbook 2002-2003 Page 296 reads: in 2000, Minera Yanacocha produced 1,795,000 ounces gold at a total cash cost of $87 per ounce. Costs were never that low before. Costs have never been that low since. Average grade ounces /ton 0.033 or 1.13 grams per ton.

My contract was to get costs down, get production up, after 3 contracts, 3 years, I had done it.

I felt it was once again time to start my own company. Do an IPO or find a shell and do an RTO. On one of my early trips to Peru, Air Canada, up graded me and sat me in the next seat to the Chairman of Placer Dome, we got talking, this resulted in me making many new connections. Also motivated me. I returned to Peru, ready to start proceed with my dream.

He said "Peru is elephant country. When you discover something big, let me know."

By the time we discovered the first "something big", Placer Dome had merged with Barrick, but the numerous connections that followed, that resulted, from that first chance meeting, were everywhere. I now knew many of the people, one must know, to be successful in this business. Most every North American, Brit and Australian, "drinkers" and "non-drinkers", the "hangers on" and the "top brass" who travel to Peru go to, spend time, the "Old Pub". Meet one and the chain starts, after a period of time, everyone knows everyone else.

The timing was now, waiting all these years, the timing was now! There where a list of reasons it was now time to do "my RTO."

The meeting of and the contacts I made as a result of that chance meeting with the Chairman of Placer Dome was only one.

The Market, the ability to raise money: The year was 2003, and this was the "first market" junior mining companies had since, the Bre-ex hoax in 1996.

There was a "dot H" company, Norsemont, available, the President was of Chinese descent. My wife is of Chinese descent. My wife asked me to help Peter, with this company, Norsemont. Peter was President, I took on the position of Chairman.

Brad Berada, a Stock Broker with one of the Vancouver Firms, came to me, said "let's start a mining exploration company, go, look for a good property, a property with potential to become a mine."

I said "If you are serious, deposit token amount, $5,000 in my Bank Account. Brad did so, I bought airplane tickets to go to Peru and circle back through Guyana and Toronto. I looked at properties in Peru and Guyana.

Both governments were in the process of privatizing properties, previous governments had nationalized, I made an offer to the Peru Government Company, Pro-Inversion. Bought and paid $70,000 on a potential property. Significant was, Rio Tinto had the adjoining property. Proved to be even more significant than I initially realized.

The Guyana Government has a bauxite mine, permitted, garage, offices, heavy equipment, haulage trucks all in place. The Government wanted $4 million for it. At $4 million it was "a steal!" My question was "do I know anybody in Toronto/ Vancouver who would finance this.

I landed in Toronto, walked the streets of Toronto, remembering my grandfathers' words, he had sold the Yellowknife Con Mine claims to Cominco, so very cheap, but he thought he did have a second opportunity. He spent time on Great Bear Lake, had uranium claims, during the early 1940 Uranium Boom. My grandfather would say, "if only, the potential buyer, had not died, he (my grandfather) would have sold more, continued to sell claims." As a teen, I thought, why did he not, then travel to Vancouver, Toronto and go up one level, talk to the people, who were financing the Buyer, who died.

Now, I was walking the streets of Toronto, it was not so easy. It is "a club". Grandfathers, get fathers into this business, who in turn get their sons into it. Regardless. Mining experience, is not the defining criteria. Mining is one business. Stock promotion is a separate and very different business.

Bottom Line: I did not find anyone to help me, buy the mine.

Ok, I had my Peru property and I was Chairman of Norsemont. I was meeting people. Paul Gill, gave me a phone call, he waned to meet. Paul told me he and Richard Gillard, had been buying up as much of Norsemont's stock as they could get and now wanted Peter out. I had taken on the Chairman's position to help Peter out and I was now being asked to help "dump him."

Paul said "We will treat him fairly, ask him if he will agree, buy all stock at a reasonable price.

There were now three of us, Directors, myself, Paul and Richard. Next Marc Levy became interested in Norsemont. This was a coo. Marc is very intelligent. Richard came to me, said "let's ask Paul to step down as President and replace him with Marc."

The first 4 of us all made millions, some of us more millions than the others, none of the 4 of us made as much money as we should have, had we know what we were doing.

Success has many fathers but failure is an orphan. This time we were successful. It takes a team.

We staked to the south of the adjoining properties, Rio Tinto and I had bought from Pro-Inversion. We staked to the north of the adjoining properties. Shortly after acquiring the property from Por-Inversion, we started negotiations with Rio Tinto. Initially we thought we would sell them our property. In the end we bought their property. Each year, the junior stock markets were improving. Previously I could not get $4 million to buy an operating mine. Now we had to get $7 million to finish paying for a property, that contained copper, but possibly not enough copper to build a mine. Marc and I travelled to London, and numerous other cities in Europe. London, RAB Capital, Philip Richards gave us the capital we needed.

Norsemont, Constancia Mine sold to Hudbay for $520, million Canadian dollars.

Today, the mine, Hudbay's Constancia contributes a full 1% to Peru's GDP. When one looks at it, I wonder would that mine be successful had I not been in the chain. How much did I contribute, dollars in my pocket say it would not be a mine today, had I not played my part.

A friend, John Plourde, as recently as last week, said "Lucky to be in the right place at the right time" There are mines, in production in Peru, Constanca, Azulcocha, Cochavara, San Vicente and still working on building more. My grandfather, Yellowknife Con Mine. When this happens over and over, generation, after generation, our contribution to creating wealth, for the employees, for the governments, and yes, some dollars for ourselves, success has many fathers but failure is an orphan.

My first job, after Haileybury School of Mines, Guy Dagenais, came to visit us, at my home in Schefferville, Quebec.

I said "I am so lucky, to have this job, so quickly after graduation.

Guy said "I believe, you have made your own luck.

There are others, that agree with John Plourde, Max Pinsky, Lawyer for Evans, wrote me, had some problem with the mention I made, of my contribution to our team effort, referring to the chain of contacts resulting from the meeting of the Chairman of Placer Dome, on that Air Canada flight years before the final sale.

CHAPTER 26

BOLIVIA

Always looking for the next one, keeps me young. I received a phone call, from a friend I made, during the two years I worked in Africa. He had now moved to Bolivia.

"Len, Bolivia is so very rich, come to Bolivia, there are gold mining properties everywhere, we need your help, someone who understands mining, someone who understands the markets." "What is it going to cost us to have you come to Bolivia."

To that time, I had never been to Bolivia. I mentioned that I had bought an airplane ticket to Bolivia, about a week before Evo Morales, became President. When Morales became President, I tore up my plane ticket.

"No Len, it not like that." "Evo Morales, now realizes he needs investment, there are opportunities for global mining people/companies here."

"It will cost you nothing for my time, if we do something, I will make my money then." "You buy the plane ticket and provide accommodations."

They agreed and I was soon on a flight to Bolivia. I like Bolivia and yes, there are opportunities in Bolivia. My first trip to Bolivia, I stayed a month, looked at a number of properties. Bolivia has a strong, well connected, Muslim community. My friends from Africa were Muslin, hence, well connected. I looked at a number of properties.

One most interesting, was in litigation, the local, previous owner, wanted the money, that would result from a sale, but wanted to continue to own the property. It appeared my friends may lose the money, they initially put up, or at least it would take some time to sort out the problem.

After a month, I left, saying "Call me, when you sort out the problem."

About a year later, my friends called me again. "Len, come back to Bolivia, we are still sorting out the problem on the copper property but we have our eye on some interesting gold properties."

I returned to Bolivia. As long as you are still alive, you never know how close you came to losing your life, but this is as close as I ever came.

I had returned to Peru, to look at these gold properties my friends wanted mu opinion on. The locals had to my friends, there was substantial gold in numerous locations. We were to look at two of them. The introduced me to the fellows, the locals who were to be our guides. I asked the Guide many questions, I was getting conflicting answers. There was plenty of gold at the bottom of a falls, coming from a glacier lake. The river runs from the high mountains, glacier lake to the jungle, but the total distance is not so great. People from the nearest village were panning gold along the river, coming from this Falls, this lake. Along side the river, near the falls, people had timbered a shaft, to get down to the pay dirt.

The biggest inconsistency was the walking distance and the supplies we needed. They told us the walking distance was 2hours, but we needed to bring tents and supplies for 2days. We were told, after you drive as far, one can to the east parallel to the river, then the walking distance would be only 2 hours. I was nearing 70 years of age, but 2hours up mountain, I can do that and back in one day.

I said, "I do not need tent, air mattress, sleeping bag, for a 2 hour walk.

The response "you must have tents, 2 air mattresses, food for 10 men, plus regular items, shovels, sample bags, those standard items."

We left La Paz early in the morning, the first night we stopped, took a hotel in a near by village. The next morning, we were up very early, still night, to push on. We crossed a bridge, the told me this is river, this is the river that contains the gold. I was told, there are miners, sinking timbered, 20 to 40-foot shafts all along the river bank, all are making a good living. From the bridge, looking up the river I could see one group.

We crossed the bridge and drove up stream, on a semi trail, that had been cut through the jungle. I did not realize, the distance we had drove. We got to a location where the vehicles were stopped, from here we had to walk, told 2 hours. We walked for 2 hours.

I said "are we getting close?"

"Oh, yes, very close?" We had now been walking for 4 hours, up mountains, down ravines, up again, up and down, up and down, there was a small steam of clear cold water, we were dry, the best water I ever tasted, we opened cans of sardines and had lunch.

"Only a short distance more and we will be there." We walked, up, up, up, walked 2 more hours straight up. I was thankful we brought 6 of the locals to carry our supplies. Now we were starting down which was to be the last downhill, would take us back to the river, just below the falls, just below the glacier lake. We arrived at the river as it was getting dark, we had been climbing up and down mountains for 8 hours. I was exhausted, my Muslim friend, even more exhausted. He was about 20 years younger than me, but he was not accustomed to this.

The locals set the tents, we two crawled into our tents, our sleeping bags, cold mountain air, fell asleep immediately.

Morning came, I crawled out of my tent, looked back up the mountain slope, we had come down, the previous evening. It hit me hard. Hit me like the proverbial "ton of bricks." I am not going to be able to climb back up that mountain!! It would take me two days to climb back up, if I was lucky.

I looked at my air mattress, I know that bridge we drove over yesterday is down there, down the river somewhere. If I throw my air mattress, in the river, with me on top will I arrive at the bridge. I know there is a Miners camp down by the bridge. I told my travelling Partner, my friend, of my plan, told my guide and the others of my plan. They thought it was a crazy plan, but also realized, I would never make it back up that mountain.

My travelling Partner thought, it could work, he decided to do the same, except he had the Locals, the Guides tie a 100foot rope onto his raft. At our location, there was an area, we could pitch tents along the river. 50feet down river, from are camp, the river walls were sheer cliffs.

We both went into the very gold glacier water at near the same time. I felt instantly frozen, was hypothermia going to set in before I reached the bridge. Before I had gone this 50feet, my air mattress, raft hit a boulder and tipped over.

Now the air mattress on top, I was underneath. The air mattress was floating on me. The rushing water was carrying me away rapidly, there was no possibility of giving up, going back to shore. I got on top my air mattress again, by turning it lengthways, under my outstretched arms, from my waist down dragging in the, water. My knees were dragging, banging the rocks, what else could I do?

I looked back, my partner was having an even rougher time than I. The Guides still had one end of the rope. Having a rope tied on him, his raft, the rushing water was pounding him again and again, against the sheer rock cliffs. He was screaming "Pull me back!" "pull me back!" Then the rushing water carried me around the bend in the river. "I could see, he did not have what it takes, to make this trip down river. I hope he was able to get back to camp." I knew it was going to be dam tough for me!

Now, I was being rushed forward, by a steep, ragging, mountain river, more rapids than river, boulders everywhere and my dragging lower body, knees were banging every rock. I had left early morning, it was now noon, how much further could it be to that camp, that bridge I saw the day before? The noon sun was warm, I did come to places where I could get out of the water for a minute, but I did not want to lose time. How far up river, had we driven the previous day, before we started walking? I had to get to the bridge before nightfall. If I was out here for the night, I would surely die of Hypothermia.

I was wet, wet, wet, dam cold. No watch but sun said it must now be about 3:00. My raft had sprung a leak, hit a sharp rock, about an hour earlier. The water had slowed down some and the river widened in areas, bend after bend, still no sight of the camp. At every location I could get out of the water, I had to stop and blow up my leaking mattress, but breathing was getting more difficult, holding the mattress with my near frozen fingers was more and more difficult with each stop. My lips were blue and fought to hold the valve stem. "Len, force yourself to blow."

It was now starting to get dark, must be about 8:00. Bend, after bend in the river. After rounding each bend, I could see some distance, still no camp, still no bridge, hallucinating, am I on the right river. Of course, I had to be. Then I rounded the corner, the bend in the river and I saw the camp. Here the river was wider and slower, the river shore had a shore line, one could walk on, some grass, mashy in places. I could see the camp, I got out of the water and stumbled along, my aching knees, that final 300 feet. The Miners seen me coming out of the weeds, they rushed to me. One on each side, propped me up, carried me into camp. This was a rough camp, these Miners make do with the minimum, but to me, it was golden. The took off my wet clothes, loaned me their clothes, which was several sizes to small, but dry. They fed me. They lit a huge fire, which I cuddled up against, blankets around me. The fire dried my clothes. After a time, I was alive again.

They drove me back to the village, now nearing midnight. By coincidence there was a bus, a typical Bolivian bus, the kind you would imagine in the out-backs of Bolivia, the bus carried people, and chickens and pigs, (young ones) and anything else people wanted to bring on board. At the many different villages along the route, people would get on and off, but the bus was always crowded. Eventually we arrived back in La Paz.

It was 3 days before I found out what happened to my Partner, when I did see him he was upset with me.

"Why did you not wait for me, in that first village."

"What?" What's the point, nothing I could do to help you along"

He was a sorry mess. I guess we were both a sorry mess, but he especially. Banging up against those cliffs the first day, had broke his fingers, that first day as I was on the river, the guides, were able to pull the rope, pull him back into camp. He spent that first day in camp, slept a second night in camp. One of the guides had returned to the Village, somehow, there was a huge inner tube, from an off-highway truck, in this village. The Guides took the blown-up tire tube to the camp. Next the cut down a number of trees and made a raft. They put this innertube on the raft, and set my partner into the inner tube. Now, they floated him down river, with one of the guides, steering the raft, by dragging, swimming, walking in the sallower areas. The Guides got my Partner back to the Village and onto La Paz.

The gold property was an interesting property, but what is called "Greenfields" During my teens, those years with Precambrian mining, I worked on "Greenfield" properties. Today Investors want "Brownfields" Properties that are already partially advanced, properties with some promising diamond drill holes. I suggested to my friends, they continue their pursuit of properties, but look for more advanced properties. It has now been a couple years, since I have been in Bolivia, but I did get a call from them, this past week, saying they now have a more advanced property with millions of ounces, gold. Sounds like I will soon need to make another trip to Bolivia.

I am presently building my next one, my next company, Lida Resources Inc. Doing the IPO shortly, hoping planning, this is my biggest one ever. Time will tell.

This process continues to repeat itself, my seventeen-year-old son, fluent in both languages, tells me he wants to be a Mining Engineer.

Thinking, sitting on this Park Bench in Banff National Park, thinking of my life, then and now. I now have 3 stories of glass, looking south, over looking Vancouver Harbor, overlooking the cruise ships come in and out, overlooking the Pan Pacific Hotel and the lights of downtown Vancouver, my husky always at my side. I am sitting on this bench, in Banff National Park, my Siberian Husky, Matilda, sitting beside me, on the bench, her head on my lap, my wife doing what women do, shopping, in the store.

My Husky and I enjoying the Sunshine. A Lady walked by, observed Matilda. She said "Huskies!" "Huskies, only recently descended from the wolf, have mind of their own, Entitled." "They know the are entitled!"

Yes, Matilda and I both, only recently, left the bush, entitled.

We Belong here!

Editors note: Donald Trump took his Father's money, and multiplied it "X" times.

My father gave me "0" money. Each month, before he passed away, I sent my father money. Does this mean I multiplied the money my father gave me infinite times?

Printed in the United States
By Bookmasters